"I think it's safe to say that Hetal has been the brightest light in the South Asian baking community for years now. Her cult classic gulab jamun bundt cake may have been the beginning, but this new book of colorful and spice-forward bakes is a whole new era! I can think of few bakers who can bring such playfulness, technical rigor, and creativity to everything they create. Crorepati jaggery caramel bars forever!"

**SANA JAVERI KADRI,**
Founder of Diaspora Co.

"Hetal Vasavada has the unique talent of harnessing the beauty and vibrancy of Indian flavors and colors into stunning and delicious desserts. I have been following Hetal's incredible journey and when they say you eat with your eyes first, they must be talking about Hetal's desserts. She can conjure the most sophisticated flavors and avant-garde techniques without losing the soul and essence of a dish. I am obsessed with *Desi Bakes*; not only with the flavors that she plays with but with the wit and whimsy of her recipes—it's a visual feast. From Gujju Bhai Toffee to Phulkari cookies, this book is a must add to any library."

**MANEET CHAUHAN,**
Chef, author of *Chaat*, and Judge on *Chopped*

# DESI BAKES

To Elara, may your life be as sweet as you. I promise
to always let you lick the "smashula" and decorate
with all the sprinkles and glitter in the world.

To my husband, Rhut, my personal forever food critic and
recipe tester. Love you and promise to make you tender
coconut pie for every birthday from now on!

# DESI BAKES

by Hetal Vasavada

*Hardie Grant*

NORTH AMERICA

# TABLE OF CONTENTS

# INTRODUCTION

One of my most favorite parts of baking is how structured and unstructured it can be. The dichotomy really speaks to both my STEM side (I am a former biochemist!) and my creative side. The precision and accuracy of baking mixed with the freedom of creativity with buttercream and cookie dough as my medium has brought me (and my friends and family!) so much joy.

In this book I really hope that you learn to embrace your inner artist and baker. The bakes in this book are inspired by Indian culture, handicrafts, arts, and experiences, but they are also rooted in American and European recipes. It's not quite 100 percent Indian or American, but a mix of both, like me!

My food styling is inspired by the vivid shades of pink, yellow, and orange, fresh flowers, and edible gold-and-silver decor you'll find at days-long Indian weddings and everywhere on holidays like Diwali and Holi. This book is filled with not only my delicious recipes but also ideas for bringing a touch of India to any celebration.

Through this book you'll see references to various handicrafts and textile styles as a major source of my inspiration. For example, I use lehariya tie dye as inspiration for my Strawberry & Mango Aam Papad (page 48), or sankheda, a lacquered wood handicraft style, as inspiration for my Filter Coffee Éclairs (page 189). I wanted to show that India is more than just paisley, peacocks, and elephants! Through my desserts, I wanted to showcase the various art forms that are found in India. Both my parents grew up in creative homes where they were taught various Indian handicrafts like beadwork, embroidery, tie-dyeing, sewing, jewelry making, and more. As I grew up, they taught me how to create these art works, as their parents taught them and so on. Handicrafts, similar to recipes, are taught and passed down through generations, changing as each generation advances and moves, but still rooted in the origin of the art/culture.

If you're new to baking, don't stress! Many of my decorations are inspired by handicrafts, and as with all handmade items, small imperfections are part of their beauty. There will be mistakes, wiggles, and squiggles, and that's okay! It's not about perfection; it's about the process and really enjoying creating edible art! Also, if you don't have the time to get to the details, there are always ways to make the designs simpler and quicker!

My dream for this book is to offer you the perfect treat for any occasion—or just because! From intensely flavored small bites to creamy custards to spectacular cakes, this book will sweeten everything from a simple home meal or lunch box snack to extravagant sweet delights for weddings, holidays, and other celebrations.

# BASIC RULES

*Baking is known for having quite a lot of rules,*
*and this book comes with a set as well!*

-------------------------

**01** Use a scale if you have one! I promise this will help eliminate 99 percent of the problems that you might have when baking! Please trust me on this!

**02** Always bake in the middle rack of your oven (unless noted otherwise). This way your bakes will bake evenly, and the hot air can circulate well. All the recipes in this book are baked using the convection setting on the oven. If you are using an oven that doesn't have a convection setting, reduce the temperature used in the recipe by 25°F (15°C).

**03** When baking multiple sheets of an item, bake them in batches rather than putting them all in the oven at once on different racks. This allows everything to bake evenly.

# OF BAKING

**04**    Do not make substitutions for important ingredients like butter, sugar, flour, or eggs unless stated in the notes. Changing the flour or amount of sugar in a recipe can upset the balance of ratios of liquids and dry ingredients and can lead to a failed bake.

**05**    Feel free to have fun with the flavors! Swap out vanilla for peppermint or almond extract. Change out the strawberries for blueberries—go for it! This is the place where you can really have some creative freedom.

**06**    Scrape down your bowls often! When making batters, make sure to scrape the bowl down as often as you can. This makes sure that you don't have any unmixed ingredients and gives you a homogenous batter.

**07**    Have fun! Baking is not supposed to be stressful: It's supposed to be fun and a way to get creative. Take inspiration from the art and crafts in the world around you and run with it!

# BAKING CAPSULE
# EQUIPMENT LIST

*Here are some things you'll need to make the items from this book. I like to call this my capsule equipment list. With these items, you can make just about anything! You don't need hundreds of molds or pans, just a few items will help you get started!*

## MUST HAVES

### Scale

If there is anything that you get on this list, it MUST be a kitchen scale. I would say 99 percent of bakes fail due to measuring errors. A scale helps make sure that the ratio of ingredients is precise and accurate. Baking is a science, and accuracy is important. With measuring cups, you can easily pack flour too tightly or too loosely into the cup and be off by 20 to 30 percent for the needed amount of flour. That is quite a bit off, and it can be the difference between a perfect cookie or a dry cookie.

While I'm on this topic, remember that measuring cups with a spout are for liquids, not dry ingredients! Put your Pyrex measuring cup away when measuring sugar, flour, or any dry ingredient! A liquid cup is different from a dry measure and can throw the recipe off as well.

I have included volumetric measurements for all the recipes; however, I would urge you to use the metric measurements instead so that you have a better chance of success! You can find scales anywhere from $10 to $50 online.

### Measuring spoons

A set of stainless-steel measuring spoons is used in every recipe. You want to have a set that goes down to ⅛ teaspoon and be sure to buy a set where the measurements are etched or carved into the handle, rather than printed on since after a lot of washes, the printed ink can fade.

### Sheet pans

I keep half-sheet (13 x 18 inches/33 x 46 cm) and quarter-sheet (9 x 13 inches/23 x 33 cm) pans on hand. I like the OXO Good Grips sheet pans. They're heavy, nonstick, and double layered for insulation so your baked goods bake evenly.

A half-sheet pan is great for big-batch cookies, and I use the quarter-sheet pan for sheet cakes, slab pies, roasting nuts, and baking small batches of cookies.

### Baking pans

A lot of my bakes use 8-inch (20 cm) square pans and 8 x 4-inch (20 x 10 cm) loaf pans since they're great for small-batch desserts. I prefer to get pans that have straight edges rather than curved edges, as they are easier to line with parchment paper.

### Cake and tart pans

A deep 9-inch (23 cm) cake pan that is light in color (aluminum) helps create light, soft cakes that aren't too brown or crusty on the outside. For tart pans, I use a 9-inch (23 cm) nonstick pan with a removable bottom from Wilton.

### Thermometer

Temperature is used to measure the doneness for many recipes. From bread to caramels, thermometers will come in handy and quickly let you know if your dessert is ready. Ideally, you want to use a thermometer pen because they're more accurate and you can take the internal temperature of your baked goods easily. Infrared thermometers work well for frying, oven temperature checks, and similar since they only take the surface temperature of objects. You can also get a candy thermometer that clips on to the side of your pot so you can keep an eye on the temperature constantly. I personally only use a pen thermometer as it works well for all cases.

## Spatulas: Offset

A metal offset spatula helps with spreading batter and frosting into even smooth layers. I suggest 4½-inch (11.5 cm) and 7-inch (18 cm) offset spatulas from Ateco.

## Spatulas: Silicone

If you're like me and need to scrape every bit of batter into the pan, then a proper silicone spatula is necessary. For small spatulas, I prefer Tovolo Flex-Core mini spatulas, and for large spatulas, I like OXO Good Grips silicone spatulas. I like these two brands because the entire spatula is made of silicone, so no worries about the head falling off of the wooden handle or it potentially becoming moldy. Also, they are heat-resistant and are sturdy enough to fold thick batters.

## Mixers: Hand mixer and/or stand mixer

I know they can be an investment, but trust me, it makes a huge difference and takes a load off your wrists and arms! In order to get fluffy cakes and tender cookies, you need a mixer to beat air into your butter or batter. In some cases, we just don't have the power or stamina to mix the batter as vigorously or as long as it's needed to get the right texture for the baked goods. You can always start with a hand mixer and upgrade to a stand mixer in the future!

## Piping tips and bags

I like to use Ateco piping tips for my decorating, and I refer to the piping tip numbers for them in all my recipes. For starters, I suggest grabbing the Ateco 787 six-piece set and one fine round tip (Ateco 2). These tips are all you need for this cookbook. Piping bags make it a lot easier to decorate your bakes. I use Ateco 12-inch (30 cm) and 16-inch (40 cm) piping bags. You can use sandwich bags, but sometimes the seams can pop on them if the consistency of whatever you're piping is thick.

## Cooling rack

Get one with a grid pattern instead of straight lines across as it better supports your baked goods. I also get racks that can fit over my half-sheet pan to catch any crumbs or drips of glaze when something is being iced.

## Other tools

- Mixing bowls
- Ruler
- Whisks
- Sieves (for sifting and straining)
- Pastry brush
- Extra-wide straight rolling pin

# NICE TO HAVES

## Silicone baking mats

These are nice to have but are not a must. You can easily use parchment paper instead. Please do not use foil (unless specified) when baking as it conducts heat differently than parchment paper and can affect the way your cakes and cookies bake.

## Spacer rings or rolling pin guides

Spacer rings are silicone rings of varying thicknesses that you roll onto the ends of your rolling pin so when you roll out dough, you can gauge the right thickness. Rolling pin guides work similarly, but they are strips of silicone or metal that are placed on either side of the dough, and the rolling pin rolls over them until the dough is the same thickness as the guides. These are nice to have and make rolling out doughs easy and quick, but you can also roll and check the thickness of your cookies with a ruler as well.

## Makeup brushes

I know this sounds crazy, but I have a set of makeup brushes that I specifically use for decorating cakes. I use fluffy blush brushes to dust berries with luster dust, eyeshadow blending brushes to pick up and add gold leaf to items, and small concealer brushes to paint cookies and cakes with food coloring. They're flexible and soft enough not to dent your doughs and can help you decorate easily.

# INGREDIENTS

## FLOUR

Fun fact: Different brands of flour have different levels of protein in them. This protein turns into gluten, which tends to give bakes a chewier texture. I like to use King Arthur all-purpose flour for cookies and brownies as it is 12.7 percent protein. For cakes, I like to use Bob's Red Mill as it has 10 to 12 percent protein, which leads to lighter cakes.

For recipes where I really want a light melt-in-your-mouth crumb, I use cake flour. Cake flour is a low-protein flour (5 to 8 percent) milled from soft wheat. Because of its low protein content, it gives you the softest, most tender cakes. You can substitute an equal weight (!) of all-purpose flour for the cake flour, but keep in mind that it will give you a slightly heavier, denser cake.

## BUTTER

Butter is the key to the best things in life, including most of my recipes. Unless otherwise specified, I use unsalted butter in my recipes. Different brands of butter have different amounts of salt in their butter, and when it comes to sweets, you really want to be able to control the amount of salt in the recipe.

Most of the recipes in this cookbook call for room temperature butter. If you forgot to leave your butter out to soften, you can add boiling water to a tall glass cup and let it sit for 5 minutes. Then empty the glass and place it upside down over a stick of butter and let it sit for 5 to 10 minutes. The residual heat from the glass will soften the butter.

## CHOCOLATE

I always recommend using good-quality chocolate for your bakes. I like using Valrhona, Callebaut, Ghirardelli, and Guittard brands. Remember not all chocolates are made the same! Chocolate chips are made so that they don't melt into a puddle in your cookies, so using chocolate chips to melt and coat cookies or cakes won't work well. For melting or coating items, I suggest using Ghirardelli melting wafers or chocolate feves.

## SALT

I use Diamond Crystal kosher salt in this cookbook. Table salt or iodized salt is finer than kosher salt. If you use table salt for your bakes, use half as much salt as the recipe states.

## EGGS

I use large eggs is my recipes. I've also included notes for substitutions for eggs in every recipe that can be made without eggs.

## AQUAFABA

Aquafaba is the water that is in a can of chickpeas. I use it a lot as an egg substitute in this book. There are two ways to get aquafaba. The first is by draining a can of chickpeas, and the second is by buying dried aquafaba powder and reconstituting it. My favorite dried aquafaba is from Vör.

When making meringues, I like to use concentrated aquafaba, which is made by boiling the canned chickpea water until it's reduced by half. This concentrates the protein and allows for the aquafaba to whip up thicker and stronger. When using aquafaba, you must use a stand mixer because you need speed and power in order to whip it into stiff peaks.

## SUGARS

### Granulated Sugar

I use granulated sugar in almost all my recipes. You can substitute it by weight with superfine (caster) sugar as well. Superfine sugar is great when making meringues, as it dissolves easily because of its fine granulation.

### Powdered Sugar

This is a combination of cornstarch or tapioca starch and powdered sugar. The starch helps thicken glazes, frosting, and icings. Homemade powdered sugar will not work in many of the recipes in this book because you need the sugar to be extremely fine.

### Jaggery

This is an unrefined sugar made from palm tree sap and sugar cane. It is typically sold in bricks that have to be grated into small pieces to be used for cooking. You can find powdered jaggery easily at your local Indian grocery store. If you can't find jaggery powder, you can buy a block of jaggery and grate it. It has a molasses-y, earthy flavor that is hard to replicate; however, you can use dark brown sugar or muscovado sugar as a substitute.

## CARDAMOM

There are two types of cardamom: black and green. Black cardamom is a large black pod that has a smoky, almost barbecue-like aroma. It's typically used in savory dishes like biryani and curries. Green cardamom is used in sweets, and it has a menthol, floral aroma. The strength of the menthol flavor and fragrance varies, depending on where the green cardamom is grown. I have found that green cardamom grown in India tends to be more menthol-forward and leans savory, whereas Central American–grown cardamom tends to have a stronger floral essence. I like to use Indian-grown cardamom (like Diaspora Co. Baraka cardamom) to make chai or pair with strong flavors like chocolate or coffee.

There are two different types of ground green cardamom. You can find ground whole cardamom, where the pod and seeds are ground together, or ground cardamom seeds, where only the seeds are ground. In this book I use ground cardamom seeds when I am referring to ground cardamom. I like to use Burlap & Barrel Cloud Forest cardamom seeds and grind them myself for strong flavor and aroma. The flavor compounds in cardamom are volatile, meaning they are sensitive to light and heat, and easily evaporate once ground. Using freshly ground cardamom means you get more bang for your buck and don't need to use as much to get the flavor you need!

## CTC TEA

The black tea used in chai-inspired recipes in this book is CTC tea (which stands for cut, tear, curl tea). It's a type of black tea that's made from the leftover buds after the tea leaves have been picked, and it's the type of tea that is traditionally used in chai. My personal favorite tea brands are One Stripe Chai Co., Chai Box, and Madhu Chocolate's masala chai blend. You can also use Lipton black tea as well.

## MILK POWDER

I use milk powder quite a lot in this book. It adds a milky, caramelly flavor to your baked goods, and it's a common ingredient in many Indian sweets! I use whole milk powder from King Arthur, but you can also use mawa powder from the Indian store as well. Avoid using nonfat dry milk powder as it's clumpy and doesn't have the same richness that whole milk powder has.

## FOOD COLORING AND GLITTER

I use food coloring a lot in my bakes to really get opaque bright colors. My go-to food coloring is Wilton gel food coloring. A little bit goes a long way, and it won't affect the thickness of your batter because you won't be adding liquid to it.

I also use powdered food pigments in my recipes. For example, I used powdered food coloring to brush on and blend multiple colors to look like a Holi explosion on my Saffron Madeleines (page 86).

You can use natural food colorings; however, keep in mind that the colors won't be as deep and will lighten as they bake.

For a touch of sparkle, I use Fancy Sprinkles edible glitter. You can add it to drinks or dust it over your desserts for a little sparkle and shine.

# EDIBLE FLOWERS

Similar to sweets, flowers are essential in Indian celebrations. They're thrown over couples getting married by friends and family, they're delicately woven through women's hair for big events, and they're used as offerings at the temple. The idea of using flowers in Indian-inspired desserts just seemed so natural.

There are tons of edible flowers, but the most important part of using edible flowers is to make sure they are grown without pesticides. Do not use flowers that you buy from grocery stores or florists! They are treated with chemicals to help them last longer that you definitely do not want to consume. Just be sure to pick flowers that are safe to eat!

The following is just a short list of edible flowers. There is a huge variety of edible flowers beyond what's listed here.

## SAVORY FLOWERS

Nasturtium

Pea flowers

Brassica flowers (broccoli, cauliflower)

Hollyhocks

Squash flowers

Dandelions

Herb flowers
(basil, rosemary, cilantro, sage, chives, etc.)

Chrysanthemums

Borage

Snapdragons

Zinnias

Radish blossoms

Kale blossoms

## MILD/FLAVORLESS FLOWERS

Marigolds

Calendulas

Pansies

Cornflowers

Carnations

Honeysuckles

Chrysanthemums

Dahlias

Lavender

Rose

Alyssum

Jasmine

Hibiscus

Impatiens

Clover

Sunflowers

Lilac

Violas

Sweet William

Elderberry

Fennel blossoms

Citrus flowers

Also, keep in mind that some flowers are more than just looks—they have flavors, too! For sweets I like to use flowers that tend to be bland or flavorless so that it doesn't compete with the items on the dessert unless I really want to highlight the flavor, like lavender or rose.

You can usually find edible flowers at your local natural foods store, like Whole Foods Market, in the herb or salad section. This is where I found a local farm, Jacobs Farm del Cabo, selling its edible flowers, and eventually I started ordering directly from them. If they aren't available in your local grocery store, consider talking to your local farmers and seeing if they can bring you fresh vegetable or herb blossoms for you to buy. Also, there are many flower growers on Etsy who sell edible fresh and dried flowers.

Personally, I like to grow my own flowers from seeds or buy plants from the store and grow them at home. I grow cornflowers, wild marigolds, alyssum, daisies, dahlias, and more! I like to "chaos garden" by grabbing a bunch of seeds and mixing them with potting soil and sprinkling the mixture across my lawn. Another added bonus is that a lot of these flowers are pollinator friendly and give bees and butterflies much needed food! In addition, you can save the seeds as the flowers dry out and keep replanting them, some even seed themselves and keep coming back annually!

You can decorate your cakes with fresh or dried flowers. To dry your flowers, pluck the petals off the flowers, spread them out on a baking sheet, lay them out in the sun for one or two days, and then place them in a dark, dry corner for a day or two. The sun helps dry the petals out, but if they are in the sun for too long, it can bleach the petals and you can lose the vibrancy of the colors. I like to use marigolds, calendulas, zinnias, roses, or any flower that has layers of petals for this drying process.

However, the petals will lose their shape if they're dried out in a pan. So if you want to keep the shape of the petals, you can press them. I suggest using flowers that have one layer of petals, like violets, violas, or cosmos. Press your flowers by sandwiching them between wax paper and placing the packet between the pages of a large heavy book for several weeks. Dried flowers can be kept in an airtight container in your pantry.

Be sure to refrigerate anything topped with fresh flowers if you don't plan on eating the dessert right away, as adding fresh edible flowers shortens the shelf life of a dish. Fresh flowers can be stored in the fridge in an airtight container lined with paper towels for up to five days.

## GOLD LEAF AND LUSTER DUST

I love using vark or gold leaf as a decoration on my desserts. In India, silver vark is used to decorate mithai (sweets). Make sure to buy gold leaf that is meant for consumption and not crafting! I get my edible gold leaf from AUI Fine Foods. I use fluffy makeup brushes to help apply gold leaf to my desserts. Same thing goes for gold luster dust: Make sure it's edible! You can add a few drops of clear alcohol to gold luster dust if you want to paint or draw with it, or dip a super fluffy brush like a blush brush into the dust and tap it onto your sweets!

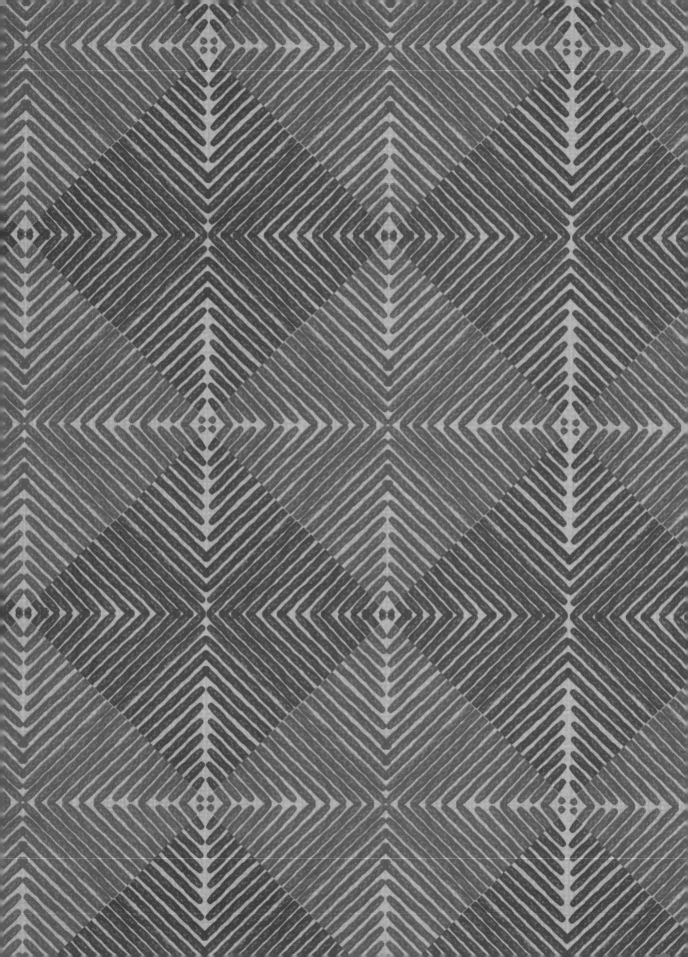

# Basics

# ROSE WATER

Rose water is an essential ingredient that is found in many Indian desserts, and it's surprisingly easy to make at home! You're basically doing organic chemistry in your own home by building a condenser using a large pot with a domed lid and ice. The rose essence is extracted by boiling rose petals in water, allowing the water to evaporate, and then condense against a cold lid and drip down the handle into a bowl in the center of your pot. You can use fresh rose petals; however, be sure to use rose petals that are organically grown without pesticides or sprays. I found that dried rose petals give you a stronger flavor and aroma than fresh roses. Also, since I'm not a fan of waste, you can use the leftover water in the pan to make Rose Syrup (page 24). The spent petals can be composted!

MAKES 1 CUP (240 ML)

2 ½ cups (600 ml) distilled water

1 cup (16 g) edible dried rose petals or 2 cups (22 g) fresh rose petals

Ice

Place a metal ring or foil ring in the center of a large, lidded pot (see Notes). Pour the water and rose petals on the outside of the ring. Place a bowl on top of the ring and place the pot lid on top upside down so that the lid handle is on the inside. Place ice cubes on top of the lid and bring the mixture to a boil over high heat. Reduce the heat to low and simmer for 20 to 25 minutes. Scoop off the water from the melted ice in the lid and replace the ice as needed. Turn off the heat and let the pot cool before removing the bowl with the rose water from the pot. Pour the distilled rose water from the bowl into a jar and store in the fridge for up to 8 months. Strain the rose petals out of the remaining water, saving the water to make Rose Syrup (page 24).

- - - - - - - - - - - - - - - - - - - - - - - - - - - - - - - - - - - - - - - - - - - -

### NOTES

- The pot lid should be domed, the deeper the dome, the better. This helps hold ice and makes the setup much more manageable.

- Distilled water helps the rose water keep longer and gives you a higher yield.

- I used Diaspora Co. dried rose petals for this recipe.

- The rose water can also be used for beauty purposes! I like to put it in a spray bottle and use it as a face mist.

# ROSE SYRUP

Rose syrup is a great way to reduce waste from making Rose Water (page 23). I use it to sweeten my coffee, chai, cocktails, sparkling waters, and more! You can use the syrup to make my Strawberry Rose Falooda (page 236). To make the syrup, you want to use equal parts strained rose water and sugar by volume.

MAKES 1½ CUPS (360 ML)

1 cup (240 ml) strained water from Rose Water (page 23)
1 cup (200 g) granulated sugar

In a saucepan, bring the strained rose water and sugar to a boil over high heat. Reduce the heat to medium-low and simmer until it has a thin syrup consistency, about 5 minutes. Pour the syrup into a clean jar and cool completely. Store in the fridge for up to 1 month.

# CHAI MASALA

Every family has its own preferred ratio of spices in their chai masala. I like my chai to be a bit heavier on the cardamom and ginger side! For this chai masala, I freshly grind all the spices before blending them together. I use this chai masala quite a lot for baking, but you can also use it to make chai (recipe follows).

MAKES ½ CUP (48 G)

3 tablespoons ground cardamom
2 tablespoons ground ginger
4½ teaspoons ground cinnamon
¾ teaspoon ground cloves
¾ teaspoon ground anise seeds
¾ teaspoon ground fennel
½ teaspoon ground nutmeg

In a bowl, whisk everything until well combined. Store in an airtight container for up to 6 months.

- - - - - - - - - - - - - - - - - - - - - - - - -

## CHAI

In a small saucepan over medium heat, add ¼ cup (60 ml) water, 1 tablespoon loose leaf black tea (preferably CTC tea) or 2 black tea bags, 1 tablespoon sugar, and ½ to 1 teaspoon chai masala and stir well. Once it comes to a boil, add 1 cup (240 ml) of milk (dairy or non-dairy). Stir it and let it come to a boil. Make sure to keep an eye on it because it can boil over! If you're using dairy milk, the milk will simmer up the sides of the pan. When it starts simmering up the side, remove it from the heat and stir. Return it to the heat and simmer the milk up the sides of the pan 2 more times (why? because my grandmother said so!). Strain the chai into your mug and enjoy!

# MANGO MURABBA

Mango season can go by quickly, so this mango murabba recipe is a great way to bottle that sweetness so you can enjoy it all year round. Murabbas are fruit preserves that were brought to India by Persians. You can find murabba across the Middle East and Asia. I like to use Kesar or Alphonso mangoes for this murabba, but if you can't get your hands on them, you can also use Manila or honey mangoes and add a drop or two of rose water to the murabba for a floral flavor! Use this recipe to make my Mango Murabba Cake (page 119) or Mango Jam Limoncello Spritzer (page 247)!

**MAKES 2 CUPS (453 G)**

1 lemon
2 cups (300 g) diced (¼-inch/6 mm cubes) fresh mango
1 cup (200 g) granulated sugar

Cut the two ends off the lemon and set them aside (see Notes). Squeeze the lemon to get 2 tablespoons of juice.

In a saucepan, combine the mango, sugar, and 1 tablespoon of the lemon juice. Add the lemon ends to the pan. Mix well and heat over medium heat, stirring occasionally for 15 minutes. The murabba is ready when it reaches 220°F (104°C). If you don't have a thermometer, you can check if the murabba is done by placing a spoon in the freezer for a couple of minutes, then dropping a few drops of murabba onto the cold spoon. Let it sit for a few seconds; if it's runny, keep cooking the murabba; if it sets, it is done.

While the murabba is cooking, sterilize a 1-pint (480 ml) glass jar by placing the jar and metal lid onto a baking sheet and baking it for 20 minutes at 200°F (90°C).

Once the murabba is done, pull out the lemon ends, stir in the remaining 1 tablespoon of lemon juice, and pour the murabba into the clean jar. Close the jar and set it on the counter until completely cool. Store in the pantry at room temperature for up to 6 months. Be sure to refrigerate once you open the jar.

- - - - - - - - - - - - - - - - - - - - - - - - - - - - - - - - - - - - - - - - -

## NOTES

- This mango murabba is made with zero pectin. Pectin helps jams set once cooled. Instead of powdered or liquid pectin, I opted for lemon butts, a.k.a. the ends of a lemon! Lemon peels have a ton of pectin, and adding it to the mango murabba will help it set naturally!

- The other factor that helps the murabba set is the sugar-to-fruit ratio. If you decide to decrease the amount of sugar in this recipe, you will have a runny, looser murabba with the texture of preserves. Keep in mind that a lower sugar murabba also won't have as long of a shelf life.

# PEAR & CARDAMOM JAM

This is one of my favorite jams to add to cozy, warm fall desserts and holiday cheese boards! I use d'Anjou pears in this recipe, but if you can get your hands on Seckel pears, I highly recommend using them as they're incredibly sweet and juicy. Make sure to use ripe, soft pears for the best flavor. Macerating the pears in cardamom sugar helps you get a deep pear flavor and allows the cardamom to meld in beautifully. If you're short on time, you can skip this step, but I promise it's well worth the time and wait! Use this recipe to make my Pear & Cardamom Bakewell Tart (page 156).

MAKES 1½ CUPS (400 G)

1 pound (450 g) pears (about 3), peeled and cut into ½-inch (1.3 cm) cubes

½ cup (100 g) granulated sugar

⅛ teaspoon kosher salt

½ teaspoon freshly ground cardamom

1 tablespoon fresh lemon juice

In a lidded container, combine the diced pear, sugar, salt, ground cardamom, and 1½ teaspoons of lemon juice. Mix well and refrigerate for at least 12 hours. The pear will release a lot of its juices, and you'll have a liquid slurry at the bottom of the container the next day.

Pour the mixture into a small saucepan and cook over medium-high heat, mashing the larger pieces of pear with the back of a spatula or potato masher, until the jam reaches 220°F (104°C), 15 to 20 minutes. If you don't have a thermometer, you can check if the jam is done by placing a spoon in the freezer for a couple of minutes, then dropping a few drops of jam onto the cold spoon. Let it sit for a few seconds; if it's runny, keep cooking the jam; if it sets, it is done.

While the jam is cooking, sterilize a pint-size glass jar by placing the jar and metal lid on a baking sheet and baking it for 20 minutes at 200°F (90°C).

Once the jam is done, stir in the rest of the lemon juice and pour the jam into the clean jar. Close the jar and set it on the counter until completely cool. Store in the pantry at room temperature for up to 6 months. Be sure to refrigerate once you open the jar.

- - - - - - - - - - - - - - - - - - - - - - - - - - - - - - - - - - - - - - - - - - -

## VARIATION

**Pear and Vanilla Jam:** Omit the cardamom and use 1 whole vanilla bean that's been sliced down the middle.

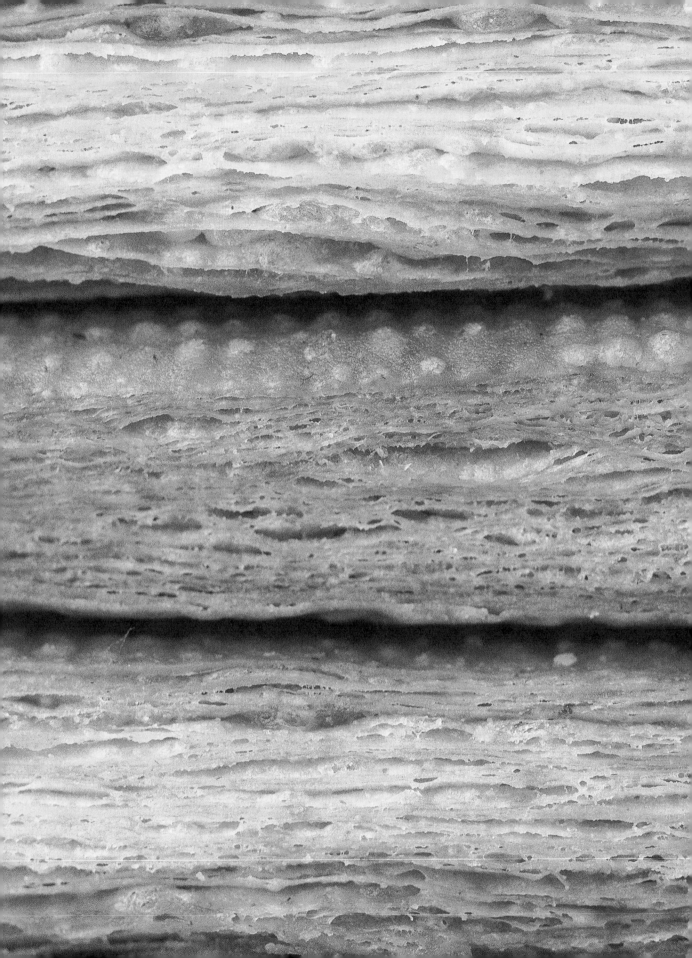

# ROUGH PUFF

This rough puff, a type of puff pastry, bakes up with beautiful layers, and I always keep a sheet of it handy in my freezer! Laminated dough, or dough layered with butter, has always been my biggest weakness when it comes to baking. It's finicky and requires lots of time, effort, and precision. Luckily this rough puff is incredibly easy to make and surprisingly forgiving. Using bread flour is key for this recipe as it's higher in protein than all-purpose flour. The increased amount of protein allows for more gluten formation, which is what creates all those gorgeous flaky layers!

**MAKES ONE 18 × 13-INCH (46 × 33 CM) SHEET**

2 cups (240 g) bread flour

1 cup (225 g) cold unsalted butter, cut into ½-inch (1.3 cm) cubes

1¼ teaspoons kosher salt

½ cup (120 g) ice-cold water

In a stand mixer fitted with the paddle, combine the bread flour, butter, and salt and mix on low speed for 30 seconds. Slowly start streaming in the cold water. Increase the speed to medium and continue mixing until a cohesive dough forms and there are no bits of dry flour. The final dough will have large chunks of butter in it. Use a bench scraper and your hands to pat the dough out to a rectangle on a clean work surface. Wrap the dough with plastic wrap and refrigerate the dough for 30 minutes.

After the dough has rested, dust your work surface with flour and roll the dough out into a rectangle that is ¼ inch (6 mm) thick. Dust off any excess flour from the dough and fold the dough in thirds like a business letter. Rotate the dough 90 degrees and repeat the process of rolling out the dough and folding it. If any parts of the dough get sticky, just pat a pinch of flour over it and continue rolling. Wrap the dough in plastic wrap after folding and refrigerate for at least 1 hour or up to 8 hours.

Repeat the rolling and folding method two more times. Wrap the dough and chill again for 1 hour or up to 8 hours.

Line a baking sheet with parchment paper. On a well-floured work surface, roll the dough out to an 18 × 13-inch (46 × 33 cm) rectangle that has a thickness of ⅛ inch (3 mm). Roll the dough up using your rolling pin and transfer it to the lined baking sheet. Place a sheet of parchment paper on top of the dough and wrap the dough with plastic wrap. If your freezer can't accommodate a whole sheet pan, you can do this step on any flat surface that will fit. Store in the freezer until ready to use.

# PIE DOUGH

The key to a good pie dough is to use cold ingredients and to touch it as little as possible! I use a food processor to quickly make my dough, but you can use your hands or a pastry cutter to make the dough as well. It just requires a little extra muscle!

MAKES ENOUGH FOR
ONE 9-INCH (23 CM) PIE

1½ cups (180 g) all-purpose flour

2 teaspoons sugar

¼ teaspoon kosher salt

1 stick (115 g) cold unsalted butter, cubed

5 tablespoons (75 ml) ice-cold water

In a food processor, combine the flour, sugar, and salt. Pulse 3 times and then add the cold butter. Pulse 3 to 5 times, or until the pieces of butter are no larger than a pea. Turn the food processor to low speed and slowly stream in the water. Stop once the dough comes together. Turn the dough out onto a lightly floured surface and shape it into a disc. Wrap in plastic wrap and refrigerate for at least 2 hours before using.

# SWEET TART DOUGH

This is the base for many of my sweet tarts. It's a soft dough that you can press into a pan before baking, no need to roll out! It bakes crispy and buttery and makes a sturdy vessel for all sorts of fillings!

MAKES ENOUGH FOR ONE 9-INCH (23 CM) TART CRUST

1¼ cups (150 g) all-purpose flour

1 tablespoon granulated sugar

½ teaspoon kosher salt

7 tablespoons (100 g) cold unsalted butter, cut into small pieces

1 egg yolk

3 tablespoons (45 ml) milk

2 teaspoons vanilla extract

In a food processor, combine the flour, sugar, salt, and butter. Pulse 8 to 10 times, or until the dough looks like coarse sand. Add the yolk, milk, and vanilla and pulse until the dough comes together. Turn the dough out onto a lightly floured surface and shape it into a disc. Wrap in plastic wrap and refrigerate for at least 1 hour before using.

------------------------------------

## MAKE IT EGGLESS

Use 2 tablespoons of heavy cream in place of the egg yolk.

# Small Bites

# PISTACHIO & CARDAMOM MUDDY BUDDIES

Gujaratis love a good handheld snack. Muddy buddies, or puppy chow, is the kind of snack you can grab a fistful of and throw into your mouth while on the move! Traditionally muddy buddies use peanut butter, but I substitute it with pistachio butter and add a healthy dose of cardamom to really make it sing. They are insanely addictive with their salty, sweet combo, making them the perfect party snack!

MAKES 7 CUPS (625 G)

4 tablespoons (57 g) unsalted butter

¾ cup (203 g) pistachio butter

⅔ cup (100 g) chopped milk chocolate

⅓ cup (50 g) chopped dark chocolate

1½ teaspoons freshly ground cardamom

1 teaspoon kosher salt

7 cups (222 g) Rice Chex cereal

2 cups (226 g) powdered sugar

In a saucepan, combine the butter, pistachio butter, milk chocolate, dark chocolate, cardamom, and salt. Stir over medium-low heat until everything is melted into a smooth mixture. Remove from the heat.

Add the cereal to a large bowl. Pour the melted chocolate mixture over the cereal and gently mix until all the cereal is coated. Pour 1 cup (113 g) of the powdered sugar into a large ziplock bag and add half the cereal mixture. Close the bag and gently shake the bag, moving it around so that the powdered sugar coats all of the cereal. Pour the muddy buddies onto a baking sheet. Add the rest of the powdered sugar and cereal to the bag and repeat. Spread the muddy buddies into an even layer and cool completely before storing them in an airtight container. The muddy buddies can be stored at room temperature for up to 2 weeks.

## NOTES

- After Diwali, if you need to use up some leftover magaz or besan ki burfi (Indian fudge-like desserts made of toasted chickpea flour, ghee, sugar, and cardamom), melt ½ cup (200 g) of your burfi down over low heat and substitute the pistachio butter with the melted burfi!

- If you want to make the muddy buddies extra celebratory, mix in sprinkles when you shake it up with powdered sugar. I like to use Sixlets or large chocolate sprinkles.

# STRAWBERRY LEMON EARL GREY TEA FINANCIERS

Financiers are my go-to make-ahead dessert for large parties. The batter comes together quickly, and you don't need fancy equipment to make them. They're known for having a rich, dense texture somewhere between a cookie and a cake and are reminiscent of a halwa. I decorated the financiers with Chantilly cream and flowers to help lighten the dessert. These go perfectly with a cup of tea or coffee. Also, you can freeze the batter in an airtight container for up to 3 months. Just let it thaw on the counter for 1 to 2 hours and scoop the batter into your mold and bake per usual!

MAKES TWELVE 1 × 3-INCH
(2.5 × 7.5 CM) MINI FINANCIERS

## FINANCIERS

6½ tablespoons (92 g) unsalted butter

Melted butter, for the pan

1 cup (200 g) granulated sugar

2 teaspoons grated lemon zest

1 teaspoon loose leaf Earl Grey tea

1¼ cups (140 g) almond flour

6 tablespoons (45 g) all-purpose flour

4 egg whites, at room temperature

1 teaspoon vanilla extract

### FOR THE FINANCIERS

In a saucepan, melt the butter over high heat and cook, stirring constantly, until the white milk solids caramelize and turn brown. When done, you'll see little brown bits in the butter, and it will have a nutty aroma. Remove from the heat and set aside to cool.

Preheat the oven to 375°F (190°C). Liberally brush 12 cavities of a mini financier pan with melted butter. When I say liberally, I mean it! Financiers love sticking to the pan!

In a medium bowl, combine the granulated sugar, lemon zest, and Earl Grey tea and use your fingers to rub the zest into the sugar and tea. This helps the lemon zest release its oils and will make a more flavorful dessert! Whisk in the almond flour and all-purpose flour until well combined. Add the egg whites and vanilla and mix with a spatula until you have a thick paste. Pour in the brown butter and mix until well incorporated.

Spoon the mixture into a piping bag and pipe the batter into the pan so that each cavity is filled one-third of the way to the top.

Bake until they have a golden-brown top and a toothpick inserted into the center of a financier comes out clean, 15 to 17 minutes. Cool the financiers in the pan for 15 minutes before transferring them to wire racks to cool completely.

CONTINUED

## STRAWBERRY CHOCOLATE COATING

⅔ cup (113 g) chopped white chocolate

2 tablespoons freeze-dried strawberries, crushed

1 teaspoon coconut oil

## LEMON CHANTILLY CREAM

1 cup (240 ml) heavy cream

¼ cup (28 g) powdered sugar

1 teaspoon vanilla extract

½ teaspoon grated lemon zest

Red food coloring (optional)

## FOR SERVING

Edible flowers (optional)

Crushed freeze-dried strawberries

### FOR THE STRAWBERRY CHOCOLATE COATING

In a small microwave-safe bowl, microwave the white chocolate in 15-second increments, stirring after each, until melted. Add the crushed freeze-dried strawberries and coconut oil and mix well.

Dip the top of each financier into the melted chocolate and shake off any excess. Place on a tray to set.

### FOR THE LEMON CHANTILLY CREAM

In a bowl, with an electric mixer, combine the heavy cream, powdered sugar, vanilla, lemon zest, and food coloring (if using) and whisk on high speed until the cream has thickened and you can see the trail of your whisk, 4 to 5 minutes. Do not overmix this; otherwise, you will end up with butter! Spoon the Chantilly cream into a piping bag fitted with a star tip (Ateco 864).

Right before serving, pipe the Chantilly cream onto the top of each financier. Decorate with edible flowers, if using, and crushed freeze-dried strawberries.

- - - - - - - - - - - - - - - - - - - - - - - - - - - - - - - -

### MAKE IT SIMPLE

Dip the financiers in the chocolate and skip the whipped cream altogether!

### SWITCH IT UP

In the financiers, change the nut flour and swap out the tea and lemon for spices! Change the freeze-dried fruit and/or the chocolate in the coating. Some combos I like:

- Hazelnut Flour + Cinnamon + Apple
- Pistachio Flour + Cardamom + Raspberries
- Almond Flour + Anise + Blueberries + Milk Chocolate

### MAKE IT EGGLESS

Use ½ cup plus 2 tablespoons (140 g) of aquafaba in place of the egg whites.

### NOTES

- Financiers are traditionally baked in rectangular pans to resemble gold bricks; however, you can also bake them in mini muffin pans.
- Financiers are great to ship out to friends. Just omit the Chantilly cream and chocolate glaze.

# DIRTY CHAI CHEESECAKE BROWNIES

Dirty chai is a chai with a shot of espresso, and it's what kept me going through grad school. The combination of chai spices, milky black tea, and bitter coffee is stellar. You can make this semi-homemade if you're short on time by using boxed brownie mix. I promise I won't judge!

**MAKES ONE 9 × 13-INCH (23 × 33 CM) PAN**

Softened butter, for the pan

## COFFEE CHEESECAKE

8 ounces (225 g) full-fat cream cheese

¼ cup (50 g) granulated sugar

1 large egg

1 teaspoon vanilla extract

1¼ teaspoons instant coffee or espresso powder

¼ teaspoon kosher salt

## BROWNIES

1¼ cups (150 g) all-purpose flour

1 cup (84 g) unsweetened cocoa powder

¼ teaspoon baking soda

10 tablespoons (143 g) unsalted butter

½ cup (93 g) finely chopped dark chocolate (about 72% cacao)

3 large eggs

1¼ cups (250 g) granulated sugar

2 tablespoons light brown sugar

2 teaspoons Chai Masala (page 24)

½ teaspoon kosher salt

½ teaspoon vanilla extract

½ cup (77 g) semisweet chocolate chips

Gold luster dust

Preheat the oven to 325°F (160°C). Grease a 9 × 13 (23 × 33 cm) pan and line with parchment paper.

### FOR THE COFFEE CHEESECAKE

In a medium bowl, beat together the cream cheese and granulated sugar until smooth. Whisk in the egg, vanilla, instant coffee, and salt until well combined. Set aside.

### FOR THE BROWNIES

In a small bowl, whisk together the flour, cocoa powder, and baking soda and set aside.

In a saucepan, melt the butter over medium heat. Remove from the heat and stir in the dark chocolate until melted. Set aside to cool.

In a stand mixer fitted with the whisk, combine the eggs, granulated sugar, brown sugar, chai masala, salt, and vanilla. Whisk on high speed for 6 minutes until thick and glossy. Slowly pour in the chocolate/butter mixture and mix until well combined. Sift in the flour mixture and mix until all the dry ingredients are incorporated. Fold in the semisweet chocolate chips until just combined.

Spoon half the batter into the baking pan and use an offset spatula to spread it into an even layer. Add dollops of each batter on top and use a knife to swirl the two batters. Tap the pan on the counter four or five times to get rid of any air bubbles and to level out the batter.

Bake until the center is set and a toothpick inserted into the center comes out with a few crumbs, 30 to 35 minutes. Cool the brownies for 1 hour and then refrigerate for at least 4 hours before serving.

To decorate, dip a fluffy brush, like a blush brush, into gold luster dust and tap the brush with your hand over the cooled brownies.

### MAKE IT EGGLESS

For the cheesecake batter, use 3 tablespoons of heavy cream or whole milk whisked with ½ teaspoon of cornstarch. Substitute ½ cup (100 g) aquafaba and add an additional ½ teaspoon of baking soda for the brownie batter.

# BLUEBERRY ALMOND SNACK CAKES

Honestly, most cakes I make turn into snack cakes in my home, but this recipe is specifically designed for snacking. Not too sweet and not too rich, just perfect to snack on! This is also one of the few cakes where there is no elaborate design, and it's just about layering all the ingredients into a gorgeous rustic cake. It's perfect to make with your little ones on a lazy Sunday afternoon or for a small brunch. Serve with chai or coffee.

**MAKES ONE 9 × 13-INCH (23 × 33 CM) PAN**

Cooking spray or softened butter, for the pan

⅔ cup (160 ml) heavy cream

1 tablespoon fresh lemon juice

2 cups (240 g) all-purpose flour

1½ teaspoons baking powder

¾ teaspoon kosher salt

½ teaspoon baking soda

10½ tablespoons (150 g) unsalted butter, at room temperature

1 cup (200 g) granulated sugar

2 large eggs, at room temperature

1 teaspoon vanilla extract

1 cup (200 g) blueberries, frozen or fresh

5 teaspoons demerara sugar

½ teaspoon ground cardamom

¾ cup (65 g) sliced almonds

1 tablespoon powdered sugar

Preheat the oven to 350°F (180°C). Grease a 9 × 13-inch (23 × 33 cm) baking pan with cooking spray or butter and set aside.

Mix the heavy cream and lemon juice in a measuring cup and set aside.

In a small bowl, whisk together the flour, baking powder, salt, and baking soda.

In a stand mixer fitted with the paddle, cream the butter and granulated sugar together for 6 minutes. Scrape down the bowl and add the eggs one at a time, mixing well after each addition until well incorporated. Add the vanilla and mix for 30 seconds. Add the flour mixture in three additions, alternating with the heavy cream mixture, beating well after each addition and stopping when just combined. Fold in the blueberries and spread the batter out into the prepared pan.

In a small bowl, whisk together the demerara sugar and ground cardamom and sprinkle it over the cake batter. Sprinkle the sliced almonds on top in an even layer.

Bake until a toothpick inserted in the center comes out clean, 35 to 45 minutes.

Cool completely in the pan before dusting with the powdered sugar.

## SWITCH IT UP

You can swap out blueberries for other berries or soft fruit like peaches or mango.

## MAKE IT EGGLESS

Use ½ cup (100 g) of sour cream and add an additional 1 teaspoon of baking powder to the dry ingredients.

# STRAWBERRY & MANGO AAM PAPAD

Aam papad is fruit leather's sweeter cousin. It's thicker and stickier and has a texture that is a cross between fruit leather and a fruit gummy. Traditionally, it's made by cooking mango pulp and/or tamarind with sugar into a thick paste, then spreading it out on a plate and setting it out in the sun for 2 to 3 days until it's soft fruit leather. To make the process a bit easier, I use an oven. I used a mix of strawberry and mango puree in order to create aam papad that looked like lehariya tie-dye (pictured on page 165), a technique from Rajasthan that involves rolling fabric up and tying the fabric at certain intervals to create a pattern that looks like leher, or "waves."

MAKES EIGHT 5 × 2-INCH
(13 × 5 CM) AAM PAPAD

### MANGO MIX

1 mango, cut into chunks and pureed until smooth

2 tablespoons plus 2 teaspoons (30 g) granulated sugar

⅛ teaspoon kosher salt

1 tablespoon fresh lemon juice

### STRAWBERRY MIX

10.5 ounces (300 g) strawberries, hulled and pureed until smooth

⅓ cup (60 g) granulated sugar

⅛ teaspoon kosher salt

1 tablespoon fresh lemon juice

Preheat the oven to 120°F (50°C). If your oven doesn't go this low, use a dehydrator instead. Line a baking sheet with a silicone baking mat or parchment paper. If using parchment paper, spray with cooking spray as well.

### FOR THE MANGO MIX

In a saucepan, combine the mango puree, sugar, and salt and cook over medium-high heat, while stirring often, until the mixture leaves a trail after a spatula is run through it, about 20 minutes. Stir in the lemon juice and pour the mixture into a cup with a spout.

### FOR THE STRAWBERRY MIX

Repeat the process as above.

Slowly pour the mango puree in diagonal lines spaced ½ inch (1.3 cm) apart onto the prepared baking sheet. Freeze the pan for 10 minutes, then pour the strawberry mixture between the mango puree lines and over the whole pan. Gently tap the pan on the counter to spread the mixture into an even layer. It should be about ⅛ inch (3 mm) thick.

Transfer to the oven and bake the aam papad for 6 to 8 hours. It's done when the top of the papad is slightly tacky and set, and the edges of the aam papad lift easily. Let the aam papad cool completely.

Use a sharp knife that's been wiped with oil to cut the aam papad into 5 × 2-inch (13 × 5 cm) strips. Roll and store in an airtight container for up to 2 months.

### SWITCH IT UP

You can swap out the mango and strawberry for any other fruit puree, but make sure to use the same weight of fruit. If you want a more chatpatta (lip-smacking)/Indian flavor, add a pinch of black salt (kala namak) and ½ teaspoon of chaat masala or Jal Jeera Masala (page 235) to the strawberry mixture.

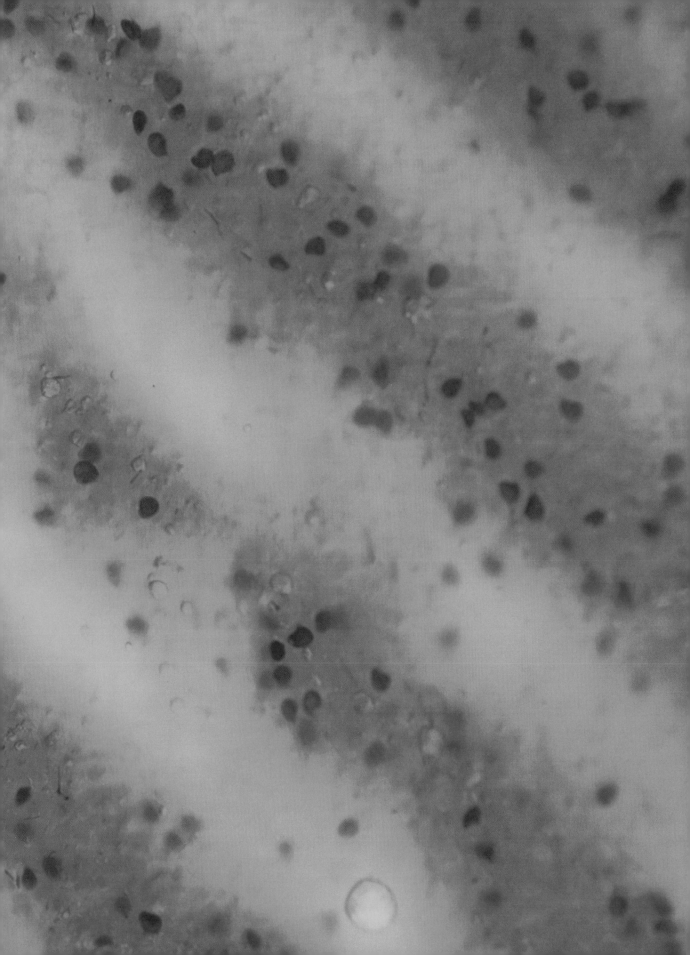

# BESAN KI BURFI CRISPY RICE TREATS

I might have danced a little when I tried my first bite of these besan ki burfi crispy rice treats. They are THAT good! Besan ki burfi is probably one of my most favorite mithai (sweets). It is made from chickpea flour that's been toasted in ghee until it's nutty and fragrant and then set with a thick sugar syrup. In this recipe, I mix the toasted chickpea flour and ghee with marshmallows. It's creamy, nutty, and simple to make! Feel free to top them with melted chocolate and an extra sprinkle of flaky salt to make them even fancier. Also, be sure to use fresh marshmallows, not the old stale ones in the back of your pantry! That is the key to getting soft gooey treats!

MAKES ONE 8-INCH (20 CM)
SQUARE PAN

Softened butter or cooking spray, for the pan

⅓ cup (64 g) ghee

¾ cup (75 g) fine chickpea flour (besan)

1¾ cups (250 g) marshmallows (vegan or regular)

¼ teaspoon freshly ground cardamom

½ teaspoon kosher salt

5 cups (160 g) crisp rice cereal

Lightly grease an 8-inch (20 cm) square pan with butter or cooking spray. Set aside.

In a nonstick saucepan, combine the ghee and chickpea flour and cook over medium heat, stirring constantly, until the mixture smells nutty and has darkened in color slightly, 10 to 12 minutes.

Reduce the heat to low and add the marshmallows, cardamom, and salt and mix until the marshmallows have fully melted. Cooking the marshmallows low and slow helps keep the final treats soft. Remove from the heat and mix in the cereal.

Spoon the mixture into the prepared baking pan and press gently into an even layer using a silicone spatula or the lightly greased bottom of a cup. Cool for 15 minutes before cutting. Store in an airtight container for up to 3 to 4 days.

# STRAWBERRY SAFFRON SLICE

Fresh strawberries paired with aromatic saffron—this is a flavor combo that is a match made in heaven! This recipe makes a snack cake that is dangerously easy to eat. I decorated the cake with whipped cream and fresh strawberries, but if you want to make it simpler, you can skip the whipped cream and strawberries altogether.

MAKES ONE 9 × 13
(23 × 33 CM) PAN

Cooking spray or softened butter, for the pan

5 tablespoons (75 ml) whole milk

10 to 15 saffron threads

3 cups (360 g) all-purpose flour

½ teaspoon baking powder

½ teaspoon kosher salt

3 sticks (350 g) unsalted butter, at room temperature

¾ cup (150 g) granulated sugar

2 large eggs, at room temperature

2 teaspoons vanilla extract

**STRAWBERRY GLAZE**

¼ cup (51 g) strawberries, washed and hulled

2⅔ cups (300 g) powdered sugar

2 teaspoons fresh lemon juice

Strawberries, for decorating

Preheat the oven to 350°F (180°C). Grease a 9 × 13-inch (23 × 33 cm) baking pan with cooking spray or butter.

In a small cup, whisk together the milk and saffron and set aside.

In a medium bowl, whisk together the flour, baking powder, and salt.

In a large bowl, with an electric mixer, cream the butter and sugar for 1 minute. Add the eggs one at a time and mix well after each addition. Add the vanilla and the saffron milk and beat for 30 seconds.

Add the flour mixture and mix until just combined. Pour the batter into the prepared baking pan and spread evenly with an offset spatula. Tap the pan on the counter to release any air bubbles.

Bake until a toothpick inserted in the center comes out clean, 20 to 25 minutes.

## FOR THE STRAWBERRY GLAZE

Meanwhile, place the strawberries in a small blender and blend until smooth. If you don't have a blender small enough, place the strawberries in a bowl and mash with a fork until pureed. In a small bowl, whisk together the strawberry puree, powdered sugar, and lemon juice until smooth.

When the cake comes out of the oven, spread the glaze over it while it's still warm, spreading it into an even layer. Cool completely before decorating, slicing, and serving.

## SWITCH IT UP

Replace the strawberry puree with passion fruit puree or lemon juice for a tart slice.

## MAKE IT EGGLESS

Use ½ cup (100 g) sour cream in place of the eggs and add an additional ½ teaspoon of baking powder to the dry ingredients.

# BADAM BURFI BARK

Badam burfi is an almond-based sweet made by cooking almond flour and a thick sugar syrup together until it turns into a fudgy treat. My badam burfi bark is unique visually, yet familiar when you taste it. It has a thin layer of fruity ruby chocolate topped with crumbled freeze-dried strawberries, gold, and edible flowers. Ruby chocolate can be found on Amazon or at your local baking store. It's an acquired taste as it has a tartness to it, which pairs beautifully with the sweet almond burfi. You can find edible flowers in the herb section of your local Whole Foods, or you can use dried rose petals.

MAKES ONE 8-INCH
(20 CM) PAN

Softened ghee, for the pan

**BADAM BURFI**

1¼ cups (120 g) almond flour

½ teaspoon freshly ground cardamom

¼ teaspoon kosher salt

⅔ cup (133 g) granulated sugar

⅓ cup (80 ml) water

1 tablespoon ghee

**TOPPING**

¾ cup (128 g) chopped ruby chocolate

2 tablespoons freeze-dried strawberries

Edible flowers, fresh or dried (optional)

Gold leaf (optional)

Grease an 8-inch (20 cm) square pan with ghee and line with parchment paper. Set aside.

**FOR THE BADAM BURFI**

Sift the almond flour, cardamom, and salt into a small bowl. This helps make sure your burfi is smooth and lump-free. Set aside.

In a nonstick medium saucepan, bring the granulated sugar and water to a boil over medium heat. Once the syrup comes to a boil, continue cooking for 2 minutes, or until the sugar syrup reaches "one-string" consistency (see Notes).

Add the almond flour mixture and ghee and stir for 2 to 3 minutes over medium heat. Spoon the mixture into the prepared pan and press the mixture into a thin layer using a clean spatula. If it feels too sticky, grease your spatula with ghee and continue pressing. Set the bark aside to cool.

**FOR THE TOPPING**

Meanwhile, in a microwave-safe bowl, microwave the ruby chocolate in 15-second increments, stirring well after each until the chocolate has melted. (Alternatively, if you don't have a microwave, bring a small pot of water to a boil and set a small heatproof bowl on top of the pot, making sure the bowl does not touch the water. Add the ruby chocolate to the bowl and stir until melted, about 2 minutes.)

Pour the chocolate over the bark and spread it into a thin layer by tilting the pan until all the chocolate spreads out over the bark. Tap the pan on the counter a few times to level the chocolate out. Top with crumbled freeze-dried strawberries and flowers (if using). Place the pan in the freezer for 10 minutes, or until the chocolate sets. Top with flecks of gold leaf, if desired, and cut into geometric shapes to serve. Store in an airtight container in the fridge or at room temperature if you use dried flowers.

## NOTES

- To check for "one-string" consistency, dip a spoon into the syrup, letting it cool for a few seconds, taking a tiny amount of the syrup, rubbing it between your thumb and pointer finger, and gently pulling them apart. If you see a single string formed, and it does not break when your pointer finger and your thumb are pulled apart, then the syrup is done.

- You can also use almond meal here, though it tends to include the almond skins. Using almond meal will change the appearance of the burfi and give it a little texture.

- Make sure to use finely ground almond flour for this recipe, otherwise the final bark will be slightly coarse.

- If you're using fresh flowers, add the flower petals to the chocolate when it's slightly cool, but not yet set. If you add fresh flower petals to hot/warm melted chocolate, the petals will wilt quickly and curl up.

- To cut the bark into clean slices, let the bark come to room temperature before cutting it. If you cut it while it's frozen or very cold, the chocolate might shatter. Use a large chef's knife and cut the bark by pressing directly down with even pressure, wiping the knife down between each cut. To get the sharp angles, I cut the bark into 3 to 4 large chunks first and then cut each chunk into smaller pieces, cutting in a different direction each time.

## SWITCH IT UP

You can swap out the nut flour, spice, and chocolate to make a variety of combinations! Here are some of my favorites:

- Hazelnut Flour + Cinnamon + Milk Chocolate

- Pistachio + Cardamom + White Chocolate

- Almond Flour + Cinnamon + Dark Chocolate

Also, if you can't find flower petals, you can substitute them with coarsely chopped nuts or sprinkles!

# GUJJU BHAI TOFFEE

When Christmas time rolls around, I always make toffee as my go-to party treat! I know it sounds crazy, but I topped this toffee with a thin layer of chocolate and a sprinkle of savory snacks, sort of like the idea of a chocolate-dipped potato chip. I use common Gujarati snacks like turmeric-roasted chickpeas, sev (deep-fried chickpea batter), deep-fried mung beans, and roasted peanuts, and it really gives off that salty, sweet (and a little spicy) vibe that'll have you coming back for more!

MAKES 1 POUND (450 G)

10½ tablespoons (150 g) unsalted butter

1⅓ cups (266 g) granulated sugar

3 tablespoons (45 ml) light corn syrup

2 teaspoons vanilla extract

¾ teaspoon kosher salt

¼ teaspoon baking soda

½ cup (75 g) chopped dark chocolate

¼ cup (9 g) sev

⅓ cup (38 g) roasted pistachios, coarsely chopped

¼ cup (36 g) unsalted roasted peanuts, chopped

¼ cup (25 g) turmeric-roasted chana (chickpeas)

2 tablespoons fried mung dal

Sprinkles (optional)

Line a baking sheet with parchment paper or a silicone baking mat and set aside.

In a saucepan, combine the butter, sugar, light corn syrup, vanilla, and salt and cook over medium-high heat until the mixture hits 300°F (150°C), 10 to 12 minutes. Remove the pan from the heat and whisk in the baking soda. Quickly pour the mixture onto the prepared baking sheet and spread the toffee into an even layer. Let the toffee cool for 5 minutes.

Sprinkle the chocolate on top of the toffee and let it sit for 5 minutes so that it melts. Use an offset spatula or spoon to spread the melted chocolate into a thin layer over the toffee. Sprinkle the sev, pistachios, peanuts, chana, fried mung dal, and sprinkles (if using) evenly over the chocolate and give the pan a gentle tap on the counter. Let the toffee sit at room temperature for 10 to 15 minutes, or until the chocolate sets and the toffee is cooled completely.

Break the toffee into small pieces and enjoy! Store in an airtight container at room temperature for up to 1 week.

# CROREPATI BARS

These are my take on millionaire's bars—*crorepati* means "millionaire" in Hindi—mixed with a Snickers bar. It's a layer of salty shortbread topped with jaggery caramel, roasted peanuts, and dark chocolate. Jaggery is a type of unrefined sugar typically made from the sap of palm trees. It has a deep molasses-y, earthy flavor that I love! I placed peanuts on the set caramel in a patterned design and poured melted chocolate on top to create an embossed metal effect that is popular in India. And since these are called crorepati bars, I, of course, had to dust them with edible 24k gold dust!

MAKES ONE 8-INCH (20 CM)
SQUARE PAN

## SALTED SHORTBREAD BASE

Cooking spray

2¼ cups (270 g) all-purpose flour

¾ cup (85 g) powdered sugar, unsifted

12 tablespoons (170 g) salted butter, melted

2 teaspoons vanilla extract

## JAGGERY CARAMEL

¾ cup (226 g) sweetened condensed milk

4 tablespoons (57 g) unsalted butter

⅔ cup (110 g) jaggery

¼ cup (60 ml) light corn syrup

¼ cup (56 g) heavy cream

1 teaspoon vanilla extract

1 teaspoon kosher salt

### FOR THE SALTED SHORTBREAD BASE

Preheat the oven to 300°F (150°C). Spray an 8-inch (20 cm) square baking pan with cooking spray and line it with parchment paper so that there is an overhang. Set aside.

In a medium bowl, whisk together the flour and powdered sugar. Add the melted salted butter and vanilla and mix well. Press the mixture into the prepared pan in an even layer. Use a fork to dock the dough.

Bake until the top is golden brown, about 40 minutes.

While still hot, use the bottom of a cup to press the crust down to compact it; this will help the bars cut well. Let cool.

### FOR THE JAGGERY CARAMEL

Meanwhile, in a medium saucepan, combine the sweetened condensed milk, unsalted butter, jaggery, light corn syrup, heavy cream, vanilla, and salt. Cook over medium heat and simmer until it reaches 237°F (114°C), 16 to 18 minutes. Pour the caramel over the shortbread base and spread it into an even layer. Set aside to cool for 30 minutes.

## DECORATION

⅓ cup (47 g) unsalted roasted peanuts

4½ ounces (124 g) dark chocolate (70% cacao), cut up

Gold luster dust

## TO DECORATE

Arrange the peanuts on top of the caramel into a linked X shape, or whatever design your heart desires! Gently press each peanut in so that the peanuts don't move around too much. Let the caramel cool completely for another 30 minutes.

In a microwave-safe bowl, microwave the chocolate in 15-second increments, stirring well after each until the chocolate has melted. (Alternatively, if you don't have a microwave, bring a small pot of water to a boil, and set a small heatproof bowl on top of the pot, making sure the bowl does not touch the water. Add the chocolate to the bowl and stir until melted, about 2 minutes.)

Pour the melted chocolate over the caramel and peanuts and tilt the pan to spread the chocolate to cover the entire pan. Tap the pan a few times so that the chocolate settles in an even layer. Refrigerate the pan for 15 minutes to set the chocolate.

Use a large fluffy soft-bristle brush like a blush brush to dust on gold luster dust until the entire surface is covered and gilded. Cut into 2-inch (5 cm) squares. Store in an airtight container at room temperature for up to 1 week.

# GAJAR KA HALWA BLONDIES

If there is a single recipe in this cookbook that you should make, it's this one. It's mom-approved (which obviously is the highest form of compliment you can get) and has all the flavors of a delicious gajar ka halwa. Gajar ka halwa is a cardamom-spiced dessert made from carrots that are cooked down in ghee and milk until soft. It's the beloved sweet by most aunties, probably because it has a vegetable in it but also because it's not too sweet.

To give these blondies the extra milky flavor that gajar ka halwa is known for, I browned my butter with some milk powder. The milk powder caramelizes and gives the blondies that iconic cozy milky flavor. I also added some cashews for a little texture, but you can omit them to make it nut-free.

MAKES ONE 8-INCH (20 CM)
SQUARE PAN

## GAJAR KA HALWA BLONDIES

1½ sticks (170 g) unsalted butter

1½ tablespoons whole milk powder

1 cup (213 g) packed light brown sugar

6 tablespoons (75 g) granulated sugar

1 large egg, at room temperature

1 large egg yolk, at room temperature

1½ teaspoons vanilla extract

¼ teaspoon kosher salt

¾ teaspoon freshly ground cardamom

⅓ cup (93 g) finely grated carrots (see Note)

1½ cups (180 g) all-purpose flour

⅓ cup (48 g) unsalted roasted cashews

## CREAM CHEESE FROSTING

7 tablespoons (99 g) cream cheese, at room temperature

½ cup (56 g) powdered sugar

½ teaspoon vanilla extract

Pinch of kosher salt

¼ teaspoon fresh lemon juice

Edible flower petals, for decorating

### FOR THE GAJAR KA HALWA BLONDIES

Preheat the oven to 350°F (180°C). Spray an 8-inch (20 cm) baking pan with cooking spray and line it with parchment paper so that there is an overhang. Set aside.

In a saucepan, combine the butter and milk powder and melt the butter down over medium-high heat, stirring constantly until the white milk solids caramelize and turn brown. When done, you'll see little brown bits in the butter, and it will have a nutty aroma. Remove from the heat and let cool for 10 minutes.

In a large bowl, whisk together the melted brown butter, brown sugar, and granulated sugar until well combined. Add the whole egg, egg yolk, vanilla, salt, cardamom, and grated carrots. Mix until well combined. Add the flour and cashews and mix until just combined. Pour the batter into the prepared pan and spread into an even layer.

Bake until the edges are golden brown, 25 to 30 minutes.

Let cool completely in the pan.

### FOR THE CREAM CHEESE FROSTING

In a small bowl, stir together the cream cheese, powdered sugar, vanilla, salt, and lemon juice until smooth. Spoon the frosting into a piping bag and cut off a ½-inch (1.3 cm) opening.

Remove the blondies from the pan and cut them into 2-inch (5 cm) squares. Pipe a dollop of frosting onto the center of each square and use a spoon to smoosh and smear the frosting gently. Decorate with edible flower petals.

## SWITCH IT UP

If you're a raisin fan, feel free to add a handful of them to the blondie batter. It adds a nice tartness to the blondies.

## MAKE IT EGGLESS

Substitute ⅓ cup (70 g) of applesauce for the whole egg and egg yolk. Keep in mind that the blondies will be more cakey than chewy if using applesauce.

## NOTE

- Make sure to use finely grated carrots so that they cook during the bake time. Otherwise you'll end up with crunchy carrots in your blondies.

# JAMUN & BERRY BARS

I've actually never been able to have a fresh jamun, but my mom would always grab frozen jamun from the Indian grocery store! Jamun, also known as java plums, are a sweet and sour fruit that are super popular in India. They have a deep purple color and almost look like mini fresh prune plums. I added some fresh berries to the mix here since jamun on their own can be quite astringent and tart. For the decoration, I piped on a simple shortbread cookie dough in a lattice pattern reminiscent of jalis, or latticed screens, that you can find all over India at palaces, temples, and mosques (pictured on page 97).

MAKES ONE 8-INCH (20 CM)
SQUARE PAN

### JAMUN AND BERRY FILLING

½ cup (67 g) frozen jamun, thawed

5 strawberries (83 g), fresh or frozen

⅓ cup (70 g) blueberries, fresh or frozen

½ cup (75 g) blackberries, fresh or frozen

2 tablespoons light brown sugar

2 tablespoons cornstarch

2 teaspoons vanilla extract

3 tablespoons (65 g) berry jam, such as strawberry, mixed, blueberry, etc.

### COOKIE DOUGH

10 tablespoons (140 g) unsalted butter, at room temperature

⅔ cup (70 g) powdered sugar

5 tablespoons (35 g) cornstarch

½ teaspoon kosher salt

2½ tablespoons (40 ml) heavy cream

2 teaspoons vanilla extract

1¼ cups (150 g) all-purpose flour

6 tablespoons (36 g) oat flour

### FOR THE JAMUN AND BERRY FILLING

In a large bowl, combine the thawed jamun and berries. Use the back of a fork to smash all the berries and jamun until it's mostly liquid. Stir in the brown sugar, cornstarch, vanilla, and jam and set aside.

### FOR THE COOKIE DOUGH

Preheat the oven to 350°F (180°C). Line an 8-inch (20 cm) square pan with parchment paper, making sure to cut it so that it has an overhang.

In a stand mixer fitted with the paddle, combine the butter, powdered sugar, cornstarch, and salt. Beat on high speed for 3 minutes. Add the cream and vanilla and mix for 1 minute. Add the all-purpose flour and oat flour and mix until all the ingredients are well incorporated and there are no dry pockets of flour.

Spoon half of the cookie dough into the baking pan and use an offset spatula to spread it into an even thin layer.

Bake until the top is golden brown, 15 to 18 minutes. Remove from the oven but leave the oven on.

While the crust is hot, use the bottom of a measuring cup to press the baked crust down. Pour the jamun and berry mixture on top of the crust. Spoon the rest of the cookie dough into a piping bag fitted with a star tip (Ateco 864) and pipe a lattice design over the berry mixture.

Return to the oven and bake until the lattice portion starts to brown slightly, 30 to 35 minutes.

Cool the bars in the pan for 2 to 3 hours. Cut into squares before serving.

### MAKE IT SIMPLE

Instead of piping on the lattice pattern, you can break the dough up into small pieces and evenly scatter them on top before baking.

# CHOCOLATE PUMPKIN SPICE PEDAS

Pedas are a cross between a truffle and brigadeiros, a Brazilian confection made with condensed milk. Whenever my mom or masis (mom's sisters) would go to India, I would always ask for chocolate peda! Peda is a fudge-like mithai (sweet) made from milk fat. In America, a lot of people use sweetened condensed milk as shortcut way to make peda. For this version, I added pumpkin puree and chai masala with an extra touch of cinnamon for a pumpkin spice feel. These pedas are much softer than your traditional pedas and almost truffle-like!

Whenever my mom would make pedas at home, she would decorate them by pressing the side of a thread bobbin on the top to get a little wheel-like imprint. I used a mini mooncake mold to get a beautiful flower design instead, but if you're feeling old school, you can totally use a thread bobbin!

MAKES 24 PEDAS

⅓ cup (86 g) canned unsweetened pumpkin puree

½ cup (171 g) sweetened condensed milk

1 cup (84 g) unsweetened cocoa powder

1¼ teaspoons Chai Masala (page 24)

1 teaspoon ground cinnamon

1 teaspoon kosher salt

1 tablespoon powdered sugar

In a saucepan, combine the pumpkin puree and condensed milk and stir over medium-low heat for 5 minutes to loosen the condensed milk and warm up the mixture. Remove from the heat and whisk in ¾ cup (63 g) of the cocoa powder in two additions. Add the chai masala, cinnamon, and salt and whisk well. Spoon the mixture onto a sheet of plastic wrap and shape the mixture into a 4 × 6-inch (10 × 15 cm) rectangle. Wrap the mixture tightly and refrigerate for 1½ hours.

In a small bowl, whisk together the powdered sugar and remaining cocoa powder. Use a small sieve to dust a thin layer of the mixture onto a plate. Unwrap the set peda mix and place it on the cocoa powder–dusted plate. Dust the top of the peda block with additional cocoa powder mixture. Be generous! Use a knife to cut the rectangle into twenty-four 1-inch (2.5 cm) squares. Roll each square into a ball using the palms of your hands.

Press a mooncake mold into the leftover cocoa powder mixture and shake off any excess. Place a peda onto a clean surface and use the mooncake mold to gently press the peda into shape. Gently transfer the peda to a clean plate. Refrigerate the pedas until ready to serve!

# Cookies

# GINGER & JAGGERY SPRITZ COOKIES

Ginger and jaggery is such a quintessential Indian combination. I grew up eating ginger and jaggery biscuits in the mornings with chai. I love the deep molasses flavor cut with the bite of ginger. This recipe has three different types of ginger in it to really boost that ginger flavor! I highly recommend enjoying these with a cup of chai or using them to garnish my Masala Chai Semifreddo (page 227) or Chocolate, Fig & Star Anise Crémeux Tart (page 141).

**MAKES 30 COOKIES**

4½ tablespoons (65 g) unsalted butter, at room temperature

1½ ounces (43 g) jaggery sugar, finely grated

1 teaspoon cornstarch

1 tablespoon heavy cream

¼ teaspoon vanilla extract

⅛ teaspoon kosher salt

1 teaspoon ground ginger

1 teaspoon ginger paste

2⅓ cup (80 g) all-purpose flour

Sprinkles (optional; see Notes)

Candied ginger, finely chopped

Preheat the oven to 350°F (180°C).

In a bowl, with an electric mixer, beat together the butter, jaggery, and cornstarch until light and fluffy, about 2 minutes. Add the cream, vanilla, salt, ground ginger, and ginger paste. Mix for an additional minute. Fold in the flour until well combined.

Fill a cookie press with the dough and fit it with the star- or flower-shaped disc. Place the cookie press flat on an ungreased baking sheet and press the cookies directly onto the baking sheet 2 inches (5 cm) apart. (If you don't have a cookie press, you can fill a piping bag fitted with a large star tip with the cookie dough and pipe out small dollops onto an ungreased baking sheet.)

Decorate the cookies with sprinkles, if desired, and some candied ginger. Freeze the cookies on the baking sheet for 10 minutes.

Bake until the cookies just start to brown, 8 to 9 minutes.

Let the cookies cool completely on the baking sheet before removing. Store in an airtight container for up to 1 week.

------------------------------------------------

### NOTES

- The jaggery should be as fine as possible. If you have large chunks, give it a quick pulse one to two times in the blender so that it's fine. Don't blend too long or it'll turn into a large clump/paste.

- Not all sprinkles are created equal! Some sprinkles will melt in the oven, specifically sugar candy–based ones like nonpareils or large hard sprinkles. I suggest using fondant-based sprinkles or sugar crystal sprinkles.

# BLOCK PRINT FLOWER COOKIES

These soft butter cookies are made with mooncake molds! I found these gorgeous floral molds online and they really remind me of block print stamps from Jaipur (pictured on page 13). Block printing is a very popular form of textile art where you use multiple hand-carved wooden stamps (blocks) to print designs onto cotton cloth. They can be extremely intricate and require a ton of hand-eye coordination. Luckily these cookies are more forgiving!

MAKES 24 LARGE COOKIES

1¼ cups (150 g) all-purpose flour

1 tablespoon cornstarch

5½ tablespoons (80 g) unsalted butter, at room temperature

½ cup (57 g) powdered sugar

¼ teaspoon kosher salt

1 egg yolk

1 teaspoon vanilla extract

Preheat the oven to 325°F (160°C). Line a baking sheet with parchment paper or a silicone baking mat.

In a small bowl, whisk together the flour and cornstarch until well combined.

In a medium bowl, with an electric mixer, beat the butter, powdered sugar, and salt until light and fluffy, about 3 minutes. Add the egg yolk and vanilla and mix for another minute. Add the flour mixture and mix until just combined.

Place the dough between two sheets of parchment paper and roll the dough out to ¼ inch (6 mm) thick. Transfer to the baking sheet and freeze the dough for 5 minutes.

Using a 2½ inch (6.5 cm) diameter mooncake or cookie mold, cut and stamp out the cookies. Be sure to flour the molds well and shake off any excess flour before stamping so that the dough doesn't stick. Return the cookies to the baking sheet and set in the freezer while you reroll the scraps to make more cookies. Freeze all the cookies for 10 minutes.

When ready to bake, arrange the cookies about 1 inch (2.5 cm) apart.

Bake the cookies until the edges just begin to brown, 7 to 10 minutes.

Let the cookies cool completely on the baking sheet before enjoying. Store in an airtight container at room temperature for up to 2 weeks.

------------------------------------------------

## MAKE IT EGGLESS

Use 2 tablespoons heavy cream in place of the egg yolk.

# PHULKARI-OS

These Oreo-style sandwich cookies are decorated with phulkari designs. Phulkari is an embroidered textile (pictured on page 97) made in Punjab and more specifically found in Patiala. *Phulkari* means "flower work," and colorful embroidery thread is used to create floral and geometric motifs across thick cotton. Phulkari textiles are used during special ceremonies like births and weddings. I use colored royal icing to create lines similar to darning stitches, which is the typical stitch used in phulkari.

MAKES 30 COOKIES

## CHOCOLATE COOKIES

⅓ cup (28 g) black cocoa powder

⅓ cup (28 g) unsweetened cocoa powder

3 cups (360 g) all-purpose flour

2 sticks plus 5 tablespoons (300 g) unsalted butter, at room temperature

1 cup (200 g) granulated sugar

1¼ teaspoons baking powder

1 teaspoon kosher salt

1 large egg

1 large egg yolk, at room temperature

1½ teaspoons vanilla extract

## ROYAL ICING

2 tablespoons meringue powder

2 cups (226 g) powdered sugar

⅛ teaspoon kosher salt

½ teaspoon vanilla extract

4 tablespoons plus 1 teaspoon (64 g) water

Gel food coloring

## FOR THE CHOCOLATE COOKIES

In a medium bowl, sift together the black cocoa powder, regular cocoa powder, and flour. Set aside.

In a stand mixer fitted with the paddle, beat the butter, granulated sugar, baking powder, and salt. Mix on high speed for 2 minutes. Scrape the bowl down and add the whole egg, egg yolk, and vanilla and mix for 1 minute. Add the dry ingredients and mix until well combined. The dough will be quite sticky. Split the dough in half, wrap each half in plastic wrap, and refrigerate for 1 hour.

Preheat the oven to 375°F (190°C). Line two large baking sheets with parchment paper.

Roll out the dough between two sheets of parchment paper until it's ¼ inch (6 mm) thick. Set the dough on a baking sheet and stick it in the freezer for 5 minutes (this helps with cutting out the cookies).

Use a 2½-inch (6.5 cm) flower-shaped cookie cutter to cut out the cookies. Arrange the cookies on the prepared baking sheets about 1 inch (2.5 cm) apart. Reroll the scraps to cut out more cookies. Freeze the cookies on the baking sheets for 10 minutes.

Bake until the edges and tops are set, 9 to 10 minutes. Let the cookies cool completely on the pans.

## FOR THE ROYAL ICING

In a bowl, whisk together the meringue powder, powdered sugar, and salt. Add the vanilla extract and half of the water. Whisk until well combined, then add more water 1 teaspoon at a time until you have a thick, pipeable consistency. Split the icing into three or four bowls and color each one with your choice of colors. Spoon the icing into small piping bags and snip off a small tip for each of them.

Pipe the icing on half the cookies in thin, overlapping lines in various geometric designs, using phulkari motifs as inspiration (see the page 81).

Let the icing dry for 30 minutes to 1 hour.

CONTINUED

## FILLING

10 tablespoons (143 g) unsalted butter, at room temperature

½ teaspoon kosher salt

¾ teaspoon vanilla extract

2¾ cups (311 g) powdered sugar

## FOR THE FILLING

In a medium bowl, stir together the butter, salt, vanilla, and powdered sugar until well combined. It'll be a thick frosting-like texture. Spoon the filling into a piping bag and cut off a small tip ¼ inch (6 mm) wide.

Flip the remaining (undecorated) cookies upside down. Pipe the frosting into a thin layer onto the flat side of the cookies and top with the decorated cookies to make sandwiches.

--------------------------------------------------------

### MAKE IT SIMPLE

You can skip the icing altogether. You can also swirl the colored icings into a container, dip the tops of each cookie into the icing, shake off any excess, and then flip and let the icing set before sandwiching.

### MAKE IT EGGLESS

Use ¼ cup (50 g) of heavy cream and 2 teaspoons of cornstarch in place of the egg and egg yolk in the dough. For the icing, you can use an eggless meringue powder (you can find one under the brand Vör) or replace the meringue powder with additional powdered sugar. Keep in mind that your icing might take longer to set without meringue powder.

### SWITCH IT UP

You can have fun with the filling and switch up the flavors:

- Add ¼ teaspoon peppermint extract to the filling to get peppermint cookies.

- Add 2 tablespoons cocoa powder and an additional tablespoon of butter for a chocolate filling.

- Pipe a ring of filling onto the cookies and then add 1 teaspoon of jam to the center of the cookies for a jammy center.

# MADRAS PRINT CHECKERBOARD COOKIES

These checkerboard cookies are inspired by Madras, a colorful plaid print that originates from Madras, now Chennai, in South India. Traditionally made from cotton colored with natural dyes, Madras has a long history that spans South India, England, Scotland, and America. This fabric was one of the biggest exports from India during British colonization and made millions for British colonizers. Over the years, the fabric has become a mainstay in everyday wear in America.

These checkerboard cookies are a bit more complicated than the typical black-and-white checkerboard cookie, but the result is worth the extra effort!

**MAKES 12 COOKIES**

2 sticks (226 g) unsalted butter, at room temperature

¼ cup (50 g) granulated sugar

½ cup (63 g) powdered sugar

¼ teaspoon kosher salt

2 egg yolks

1 teaspoon vanilla extract

¼ teaspoon ground cardamom

2⅓ cups (280 g) all-purpose flour

Pink, yellow, and orange gel food coloring

1 egg white, for assembly

In a bowl, with an electric mixer, beat the butter, granulated sugar, powdered sugar, and salt on high speed for 1 minute. Add the egg yolks, vanilla, and cardamom and mix for 1 minute. Add the flour and mix until just combined.

Split the dough into 2 equal portions (about 325 g each). Split 1 of the portions into 3 portions (about 108 g each). Combine 2 of those small portions into a dough ball. You should have 1 large portion (about 325 g), 1 medium portion (about 216 g), and 1 small portion (about 108 g).

To the large portion, add pink food coloring and use your hands to gently knead the color into the cookie dough mix until the color is incorporated. Shape the dough into a 6 × 9-inch (15 × 23 cm) rectangle. Wrap tightly with plastic wrap.

To the medium portion, add yellow food coloring and mix until the color is fully incorporated. Shape the dough into a 6-inch (15 cm) square and wrap in plastic wrap.

To the small portion, add the orange food coloring and mix until the color is fully incorporated. Shape the dough into a 6 × 3-inch (15 × 7.5 cm) rectangle and wrap in plastic wrap.

Freeze all the dough rectangles for 15 minutes.

Remove the dough from the freezer. Cut the pink dough into three 6 × 3-inch (15 × 7.5 cm) rectangles. Cut the yellow dough into two 6 × 3-inch (15 × 7.5 cm) rectangles. Make 2 stacks of dough with 3 rectangles in each: For one, make a stack of yellow/pink/yellow. For the second stack, make a stack of pink/orange/pink. Lightly brush egg white in between the layers to help stick them together.

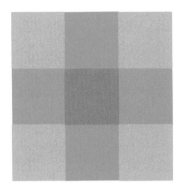

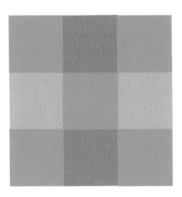

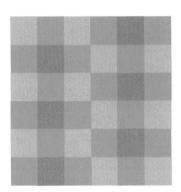

Trim the edges of the stacked doughs so that they are even, then slice each stack lengthwise into strips ½ inch (1.3 cm) wide. Lightly brush the wide side of the yellow/pink/yellow dough with egg white and stack a strip of pink/orange/pink dough on top, and then add another slice of the yellow/pink/yellow dough so that it matches the first two images. You should have 2 logs of each pattern.

Cut each log in half crosswise and combine the logs, using egg whites to glue them together, to create the final pattern.

Place the log of checkerboard cookie dough onto a baking sheet and freeze for 20 minutes.

Preheat the oven to 350°F (180°C). Line a baking sheet with parchment paper or a silicone baking mat.

Slice the log into cookies ¼ inch (6 mm) thick and arrange on the prepared baking sheet 2 inches (5 cm) apart.

Bake until the edges just begin to brown, 13 to 15 minutes. You don't want too much color on these cookies.

Let the cookies cool completely on the baking sheets. Store in an airtight container for up to 2 weeks.

-------------------------------------------------------------

## MAKE IT EGGLESS

Use ¼ cup (60 ml) heavy cream in place of the egg yolks in the dough. Use water instead of egg white when assembling the logs. FYI: The cookies will spread a little as there is no egg protein to help keep their shape.

# SAFFRON MADELEINES

Madeleines are made with a sponge cake batter, but they are still generally considered cookies. You can serve these dusted with powdered sugar; or, if you're feeling a little extra, you can coat them in a thin shell of chocolate! I suggest using Ghiradelli white chocolate melting wafers as they're made to melt easily and then harden into a shiny shell. Madeleines are best served the day they're baked since they tend to dry out quickly! To make this, you will need a 12-cavity madeleine pan. To make these eggless, use ⅓ cup (70 g) aquafaba in place of the whole egg and egg yolk and add 1 teaspoon of cornstarch to the dry ingredients.

MAKES 12 MADELEINES

## SAFFRON MADELEINES

½ cup (60 g) all-purpose flour

⅛ teaspoon kosher salt

¼ teaspoon baking powder

¼ cup (50 g) granulated sugar

2 teaspoons honey

1 large egg, at room temperature

1 large egg yolk, at room temperature

4 tablespoons (57 g) unsalted butter, melted

5 or 6 saffron threads

Melted butter, for the madeleine pan

## WHITE CHOCOLATE SHELL

½ cup (85 g) white chocolate melting wafers

Powdered food coloring (orange and pink)

Gold leaf

### FOR THE SAFFRON MADELEINES

In a small bowl, whisk together the flour, salt, and baking powder.

In a stand mixer fitted with the whisk, beat the sugar, honey, whole egg, and egg yolk until the mixture is pale, thick, and fluffy, 2 to 3 minutes. Sift the dry ingredients over the mixture and then fold in until just combined. Add the melted butter and saffron and gently fold until well incorporated. Pour the batter into a piping bag and refrigerate for at least 4 hours or overnight.

When ready to bake, brush melted butter into the cavities of the madeleine pan and freeze the pan while your oven preheats. Preheat the oven to 425°F (220°C).

Pipe 1 tablespoon of batter into each cavity (about 21 g each). The batter will spread out on its own while it bakes, so there is no need to spread it.

Bake the madeleines for 2 minutes. Reduce the oven temperature to 400°F (200°C) and bake until the edges turn golden brown, another 4 to 5 minutes.

Let the madeleines cool for 5 minutes in the pan before turning them out onto a wire rack.

### FOR THE WHITE CHOCOLATE SHELL

In a microwave-safe bowl, microwave the chocolate in 15-second increments, stirring well after each until the chocolate has melted. (Alternatively, if you don't have a microwave, bring a small pot of water to a boil and set a small heatproof bowl on top of the pot, making sure the bowl does not touch the water. Add the chocolate to the bowl and stir until melted, about 2 minutes.)

Wipe down the madeleine pan and pipe 2 to 3 teaspoons of white chocolate into each cavity. Gently press each madeleine shell face down into the chocolate. Refrigerate the pan for 5 to 10 minutes, or until the chocolate sets. Remove each madeleine from the pan.

Take a small fluffy brush like a blush brush and lightly dip it into the pink powdered food coloring. Brush and buff the color onto the chocolate, leaving some white spaces. Repeat with the orange powder in the white spaces. Blend the pink and orange so that it looks seamless. Use a small brush to add gold leaf.

# LEMON CORIANDER SNICKERDOODLES

I know coriander sounds weird in a cookie, but trust me, it works. This flavor was inspired by nimbu pani ("lemon water"), my favorite Indian sharbat (drink). My mom adds fennel, cumin, and a touch of coriander to her nimbu pani and I love it! The coriander adds a floral, citrus aroma and flavor that really complements the lemon in this recipe.

The key to soft, chewy snickerdoodles is to bake them just enough so they don't brown and then let the cookie continue baking on the hot baking sheet out of the oven. It'll look raw or not set, but trust me, it'll be the perfect texture once they're cooled! Also, these snickerdoodles are BIG—4 to 5 inches (10 to 13 cm) wide. If you want to make the cookies smaller, bake them for 1 to 2 minutes less than the recipe below so that you still have soft, chewy cookies!

MAKES 24 LARGE COOKIES

## SNICKERDOODLES

4¾ cups (570 g) all-purpose flour

2 tablespoons baking powder

1 teaspoon kosher salt

2¼ cups (450 g) granulated sugar

2½ tablespoons (15 g) grated lemon zest

3 sticks (350 g) unsalted butter, at room temperature

2 teaspoons vanilla extract

½ cup (120 ml) heavy cream

Yellow food coloring

### FOR THE SNICKERDOODLES

In a small bowl, whisk together the flour, baking powder, and salt. Set aside.

In the bowl of a stand mixer, combine the sugar and lemon zest. Rub the lemon zest and sugar together using your fingertips until the sugar is pale yellow and clumpy. Snap on the paddle, add the butter, and mix for 3 minutes. Add the vanilla and heavy cream and mix for 1 minute. Add the flour mixture and mix on low speed until everything is incorporated.

Split the dough in half and add yellow food coloring to one half of the dough and mix until the dough has one even color. Cover and refrigerate the dough for 1 hour.

Preheat the oven to 375°F (190°C). Line two or more baking sheets with parchment paper.

CONTINUED

## CORIANDER SUGAR

2 teaspoons coriander seeds

2 tablespoons granulated sugar

### FOR THE CORIANDER SUGAR

Roughly grind the coriander using a mortar and pestle. Whisk the ground coriander with the sugar and set aside.

Roll the white dough into 2-tablespoon (30 g) balls. Do the same for the yellow dough. Grab 1 ball of yellow dough and 1 of white dough, smush them together, and roll it into one big ball. Repeat until you have 24 large balls. Roll each ball into the coriander sugar and arrange 6 of them on each lined baking sheet spaced about 3 inches (7.5 cm) inches apart. Freeze the cookies for 5 minutes.

Bake until the edges start to take on a little color, 9 to 11 minutes. The cookies will be soft but will continue to cook on the hot baking sheet.

Let the cookies cool completely on the baking sheet. Move the baked cookies onto a rack and bake the rest of the cookies.

Store in an airtight container at room temperature for up to 1 week.

- - - - - - - - - - - - - - - - - - - - - - - - - - - - - - - - - - - - - - - - - - - - - - - - - - -

### SWITCH IT UP

The coriander sugar can be swapped for another spice and sugar combo, or you could use citrus zest for a flavor change! Here are some combos I love:

- Chai masala + demerara sugar
- Lemon zest + cardamom
- Lime zest + unsweetened shredded coconut

# ANISE & ALMOND VIENNESE COOKIES

Like most Asian kids, I would always get excited when I saw a tin of Royal Dansk butter cookies at home, which was sadly almost always filled with sewing materials. The buttery biscuits from those classic tins were the inspiration for these cookies. This cookie dough comes together in seconds; it's a one-bowl recipe! If you're not a fan of anise, feel free to substitute it with cardamom, cinnamon, chai masala, or whatever spice you like. I dipped each cookie into melted chocolate mixed with roasted almonds to add a little crunch. I suggest buying Ghiradelli milk or dark chocolate melting wafers; they taste great and don't need to be tempered to set.

MAKES 30 COOKIES

2 sticks (226 g) unsalted butter, at room temperature

7 ½ tablespoons (52 g) powdered sugar

7 ½ tablespoons (52 g) cornstarch

½ teaspoon ground anise

½ teaspoon kosher salt

1 teaspoon vanilla extract

1¾ cups (210 g) all-purpose flour

4 ounces (115 g) chocolate melting wafers

3 tablespoons (28 g) unsalted roasted almonds, finely chopped

Gold leaf (optional)

Preheat the oven to 350°F (180°C). Line a baking sheet with parchment paper or a silicone baking mat.

In a bowl, stir together the butter, powdered sugar, cornstarch, anise, salt, and vanilla until well combined. Add the flour and mix until just combined and there are no dry bits of flour in the cookie dough. Refrigerate the cookie dough for 10 minutes.

Spoon the cookie dough into a piping bag fitted with a large star tip. Pipe lines 3 inches (7.5 cm) long about 1 inch (2.5 cm) apart onto the prepared baking sheet.

Bake the cookies until the edges JUST start to brown, 12 to 14 minutes. You do not want too much color on these cookies! Let the cookies cool completely on the baking sheet.

While the cookies are cooling, in a microwave-safe bowl, melt the chocolate in 15-second increments, stirring well after each. Add the chopped roasted almonds and stir until well mixed.

Dip half of each cookie into the melted chocolate and shake off any excess. Refrigerate the cookies for 5 minutes to set the chocolate. Brush on some gold leaf if you like. Store in an airtight container for up to 5 days.

- - - - - - - - - - - - - - - - - - - - - - - - - - - - - - - - - - - - - - - - - -

**NOTE**

• To make it gluten-free, substitute the flour with 1:1 gluten-free pastry flour and add ¼ teaspoon of xanthan gum to the dry ingredients.

# CARDAMOM & BROWN BUTTER SANDWICH COOKIES

When I gave these cookies to my husband, Rhut, to try while I was testing them, he said they tasted like the Dutch butter cookies in those blue tins. To be honest, he wasn't too far off. The brown butter frosting really gives these cookies a butteriness and butterscotch-like flavor. You could also skip the filling and just make the cookies if you want to serve more people or make this recipe simpler!

MAKES 12 COOKIES

## CARDAMOM COOKIES

1½ cups (180 g) all-purpose flour

½ teaspoon ground cardamom

¼ teaspoon kosher salt

1 stick (113 g) unsalted butter, at room temperature

¼ cup (50 g) granulated sugar

3 tablespoons (42 g) dark brown sugar

2 tablespoons powdered sugar

2 tablespoons applesauce

2 tablespoons heavy cream

¼ teaspoon vanilla extract

## FOR THE CARDAMOM COOKIES

Preheat the oven to 350°F (180°C). Line a large baking sheet with parchment paper.

In a medium bowl, whisk together the flour, cardamom, and salt.

In a bowl, with an electric mixer, cream together the butter, granulated sugar, brown sugar, and powdered sugar on high speed for 1 minute. Scrape down the bowl and add the applesauce, cream, and vanilla and mix until well combined. Scrape down the bowl once again. Add the flour mixture to the sugar mixture and mix until just combined.

Roll the dough out between two large pieces of parchment paper until it is ¼ inch (6 mm) thick. Set on a baking sheet and freeze for 10 minutes.

Use a 3-inch (7.5 cm) square scalloped cookie cutter to cut out cookies and arrange them on the baking sheet 1 inch (2.5 cm) apart. Reroll the scraps to cut out more cookies. Freeze all the cookies for 10 minutes. This ensures that the cookies keep their shape.

Bake the cookies until the edges just start to brown, 10 to 12 minutes.

Let cool for 5 minutes on the baking sheet and then transfer to a wire rack.

CONTINUED

### BROWN BUTTER FROSTING

7½ tablespoons (106 g) unsalted butter

1 cup (113 g) powdered sugar

2 teaspoons milk

¼ teaspoon vanilla extract

### OPTIONAL DECORATION

2 tablespoons melted chocolate

Chopped pistachios

Edible flower petals

### FOR THE BROWN BUTTER FROSTING

Meanwhile, in a saucepan, stir the butter over medium-high heat for 5 to 10 minutes. The butter will melt and start bubbling. Continuously stir the mixture until the milk solids starts to caramelize, you see little brown specks in your pan, and it starts to smell nutty. Remove from the heat and set aside for 10 minutes. Pop the brown butter into the freezer for 15 minutes to help solidify it.

In a bowl, whisk together 6½ tablespoons (90 g) of the brown butter, the powdered sugar, milk, and vanilla until well combined with a smooth frosting-like mixture. You want the thickness to be the same as buttercream.

There are two ways to assemble the cookies. You can use a table knife to spread the filling or use a piping bag (or small plastic bag) to pipe the filling onto the cookies. Flip half of the cookies over and spread/pipe the filling onto them. Top with the remaining cookies.

If desired, decorate the cookies with a drizzle of melted chocolate and a sprinkle of pistachios and edible flower petals.

Store in an airtight container in the fridge for up to 1 week.

# FLOWER GARLAND COOKIES

This is one of those Willy Wonka ideas that popped into my head when I was in India, walking in the flower markets near the temples. I wanted to re-create the texture, colors, and aroma of the flower garlands but with sugar cookies! I give the cookies shape by baking them over a silicone semispherical mold, though you could bake them over cupcake pans or balls of foil. If you don't plan to turn them into a garland, you can also just bake them flat on a baking sheet.

MAKES 36 TO 48 COOKIES

4¾ cups (570 g) all-purpose flour

2¼ teaspoons baking powder

¾ teaspoon kosher salt

1½ cups (300 g) granulated sugar

3 sticks (340 g) unsalted butter, at room temperature

1 large egg, at room temperature

1 teaspoon vanilla extract

1 teaspoon rose water, store-bought or homemade (page 23)

Pink, purple, orange, and yellow gel food coloring

In a bowl, whisk together the flour, baking powder, and salt until well combined.

In a stand mixer fitted with the paddle, cream the sugar and butter until fluffy and pale, about 5 minutes. Scrape down the bowl and add the egg, vanilla, and rose water and mix for 2 minutes. Add the flour mixture and mix on low until well combined.

Split the dough into 4 equal portions. Gently knead a few drops of food coloring gel into each piece to make pink, purple, orange, and yellow dough. Shape each dough ball into a disc and wrap in plastic wrap. Refrigerate for at least 1 hour.

Preheat the oven to 325°F (160°C). Line a baking sheet with parchment paper if making flat cookies.

To marble the dough, break up the yellow and orange dough and randomly place chunks of each color onto parchment paper. Shape the chunk into a rectangle. Place parchment paper on top and gently roll the dough out until it is ¼ inch (6 mm) thick. Place in the freezer for 5 minutes. Cut the cookies out with a flower-shaped cookie cutter—2- to 3-inch (5 to 7.5 cm) cutters work best. Use a drinking straw to cut out a small hole in the center of each cookie. Reroll the scraps and cut out more cookies. Repeat the process with the pink and purple doughs.

If making flat cookies, arrange the cookies on the baking sheet 2 inches (5 cm) apart. Freeze the sheet for 10 minutes; this is important so the cookies keep their shape. If making rounded cookies, flip a silicone semispherical mold upside down. Place a cookie on top of each dome and freeze for 10 minutes before baking.

Bake until the cookies look set, 7 to 9 minutes, being careful to get any color on the cookies. Let the cookies cool for 10 minutes on the baking sheet or mold, then gently remove and cool completely on a rack.

To make the garland, tie a large knot at one end of a length of a thick yarn and thread the cookies onto the yarn. Use them to decorate your dessert table. Store in an airtight container for up to 4 days.

- - - - - - - - - - - - - - - - - - - - - - - - - - - - - - - - - - -

## MAKE IT EGGLESS

Use 3 tablespoons (42 g) of heavy cream in place of the egg. The cookies will spread a bit if making them eggless.

# PASSION FRUIT SHORTBREAD COOKIES

Walker's shortbread biscuits were a luxury in my household. Buttery, slightly salty, and perfect dunked in a glass of warm, milky chai. These shortbread cookies have a special ingredient in them—milk powder. The milk powder adds a creamy flavor that pairs well with tart passion fruit. Now I know finding passion fruit can be hard, so feel free to substitute key limes, lemons, or any other citrus for the passion fruit!

MAKES 16 COOKIES

## SHORTBREAD COOKIES

14 tablespoons (200 g) unsalted butter, at room temperature

1 cup (113 g) powdered sugar

1 tablespoon whole milk powder

¾ teaspoon kosher salt

2¼ teaspoons vanilla extract

7 tablespoons (39 g) almond flour

2 cups (240 g) all-purpose flour

## PASSION FRUIT GLAZE

½ cup (60 g) powdered sugar

2½ teaspoons passion fruit pulp

Edible flowers (optional)

## FOR THE SHORTBREAD COOKIES

Preheat the oven to 300°F (150°C).

In a stand mixer fitted with the paddle, cream the butter, powdered sugar, milk powder, salt, and vanilla for 2 minutes on medium speed. Scrape down the bowl and add the almond flour and mix for 1 minute on high speed. Add the all-purpose flour and mix just until all the flour has been incorporated.

Spoon the dough into a 9-inch (23 cm) round cake pan. Since the dough is very sticky, pop the pan in the freezer for 15 minutes. Lay a sheet of plastic wrap on top and press the dough into an even layer into the bottom of the pan. Remove the plastic wrap and dock the dough with a fork.

Bake until golden brown, 35 to 45 minutes.

Let the shortbread cool in the pan for 10 minutes before cutting into 16 wedges. Make sure to the cut the cookies while they are warm!

## FOR THE PASSION FRUIT GLAZE

In a small bowl, stir the powdered sugar and passion fruit pulp until well combined. Spoon the glaze on top of the cookies. If you'd like, sprinkle with edible flowers. (I used dried marigold and calendula petals.) Let the glaze set before serving.

# PINEAPPLE LIME KISSES

These cookies are so bright and colorful. They remind me of Diwali decorations and rangoli! Rangoli are bright and colorful designs made by using colored powders, rice, and/or flowers. They are carefully arranged in platters or on the floor to create symmetrical mandalas, peacocks, and other Indian motifs. Rangolis are added as decorative elements to your home during big holidays like Holi, Diwali, or Navratri! The beauty of rangoli is that it's never permanent, and it's to be enjoyed while it's there, kind of like cake!

MAKES 3 DOZEN COOKIES

## LIME COOKIES

½ cup plus 1½ tablespoons (117 g) granulated sugar

1 teaspoon grated lime zest

9 tablespoons (128 g) unsalted butter, at room temperature

3½ tablespoons (49 g) cream cheese, at room temperature

2 teaspoons heavy cream

½ teaspoon fresh lime juice

¼ teaspoon kosher salt

½ teaspoon vanilla extract

¾ teaspoon cornstarch

1⅔ cups (200 g) all-purpose flour

Gel food coloring

## PINEAPPLE FILLING

1 tablespoon unsalted butter, at room temperature

2 teaspoons pineapple juice

½ cup (60 g) powdered sugar

Pinch of salt

## FOR THE LIME COOKIES

Preheat the oven to 350°F (180°C). Line two baking sheets with parchment paper or silicone baking mats.

In the bowl of a stand mixer, combine the sugar and lime zest and use your hands to rub the zest into the sugar for 1 minute. The sugar will start to look a little wet and get fragrant. Snap on the paddle, add the butter and cream cheese, and mix on high speed for 3 minutes. Add the heavy cream, lime juice, salt, vanilla, and cornstarch and mix for 1 minute. Add the flour and mix until just combined.

Divide the dough into 3 equal portions and place each portion in a separate bowl. Add a different food coloring to each bowl and gently fold until you have an even color. I used rose, red, and yellow gel food coloring.

Lay a sheet of plastic wrap on your work surface and spoon the cookie dough into thick rows touching each other. Roll the dough up in the plastic wrap so you have a log of cookie dough. Twist the ends of the plastic wrap (like a giant candy wrapper) and cut one end off at the point where the cookie dough starts. Drop the log with the cut side down into a piping bag fitted with a star tip (Ateco 864).

Pipe 1-inch (2.5 cm) dollops onto the prepared baking sheets about 2 inches (5 cm) apart.

Bake the cookies, one sheet at a time, until the cookies are set and look like they are going to start taking on color, 8 to 10 minutes, making sure that they don't brown.

Let the cookies cool completely on the pan.

### FOR THE PINEAPPLE FILLING

In a bowl, stir together the butter, pineapple juice, powdered sugar, and salt into a smooth frosting. Spoon the filling into a piping bag and snip off a ¼-inch (6 mm) tip.

Pair up the completely cooled cookies and pipe a dollop of pineapple filling onto half of them. Top with the other half of the cookies and serve.

# Cakes

# LEMON CARDAMOM PISTACHIO TORTE

Tortes are the perfect tea cake. They're not too sweet, and they're light, moist, and delicate! A torte is a cake made with nut flours—in this case, pistachio. This cake plays on the flavors of pista burfi, pistachio fudge spiced with cardamom, with a summery twist. I used a peacock stencil to create a gorgeous design that's reminiscent of a block print! You can buy stencils or cut your own out of parchment paper. Also, this is another aunty-approved dessert; make this on your next holiday, and you'll be getting major brownie points! Enjoy with tea or coffee.

**MAKES ONE 9-INCH (23 CM) ROUND CAKE**

Softened butter, for the pan

¾ cup (180 g) whole milk

1 teaspoon vanilla extract

1½ tablespoons fresh lemon juice

1 cup (108 g) unsalted roasted pistachios

1¼ cups (150 g) cake flour

1 cup (200 g) granulated sugar

1 teaspoon grated lemon zest

7 tablespoons (100 g) unsalted butter, at room temperature

3 tablespoons (42 g) coconut oil

½ teaspoon freshly ground cardamom

1 teaspoon baking powder

½ teaspoon baking soda

¼ teaspoon kosher salt

2 large eggs at room temperature

2 tablespoons powdered sugar, for dusting

Preheat the oven to 325°F (160°C). Grease and line a 9-inch (23 cm) round cake pan with a round of parchment paper.

In a large cup, whisk together the milk, vanilla, and lemon juice and set aside.

In a blender, process the pistachios until you have a fine pistachio flour. You don't want any large pieces of pistachios in the batter. Measure out 2 tablespoons of the pistachio flour and set aside. Transfer the rest of the pistachio flour to a medium bowl and whisk in the cake flour.

In the bowl of a stand mixer bowl, combine the granulated sugar and lemon zest and rub the zest into the sugar until the sugar is aromatic and looks slightly wet, about 1 minute. Snap on the paddle and beat the butter, coconut oil, cardamom, baking powder, baking soda, and salt on high for 6 minutes, making sure to scrape down the sides halfway through. Add the eggs one at a time, mixing for 30 seconds after each addition. Alternate adding the flour mixture and milk mixture in three additions, beginning and ending with the flour and mixing after each addition using a spatula. Pour the batter into the prepared pan and tap on the counter 4 to 5 times to get rid of any air bubbles and even out the batter.

Bake until a toothpick inserted in the center comes out clean, 35 to 40 minutes.

Cool completely in the pan before turning the cake out onto a serving plate.

To decorate, dust the cake with powdered sugar. Gently place a stencil (see headnote) on top and dust the reserved pistachio flour on top of the cake. Store in an airtight container at room temperature for up to 3 days.

## MAKE IT EGGLESS

Use 2 tablespoons of vegan mayonnaise and 3 tablespoons (42 g) of sour cream in place of the eggs.

# SALAM PAK SPICE CAKE

In the winters, you can find salam pak being made in mithai (sweet) shops in Surat. Salam pak is a fudgy sweet made of a ton of different spices and herbs that also has medicinal value. It includes the medicinal plant salam panja, which is supposed to support your immune system, along with ingredients such as chestnut flour, ginger, nutmeg, mace, and an ungodly amount of ghee. When I had it for the first time, it reminded me of a spicy gingerbread. This recipe has some of the main ingredients from salam pak but with a brown butter frosting.

I decorated the cake to look like a kantha quilt (pictured on page 164). Kantha quilts are hand-stitched quilts (thus the messy stitches on the cake!) made from cotton or recycled saris. They're popularly made in Rajasthan, where they are sewn from block-printed cotton. It's a great way to use up scraps of fabric leftover from other projects, making it a no-waste handicraft!

MAKES ONE 9 × 13-INCH
(23 × 33 CM) CAKE

## SALAM PAK SPICE CAKE

Softened butter or cooking spray,
for the pan

3 cups (360 g) cake flour

1½ teaspoons baking soda

1 tablespoon Chai Masala (page 24)

½ teaspoon ground ginger

¼ teaspoon ground mace

1 teaspoon kosher salt

9 tablespoons (128 g) unsalted
butter, at room temperature

2 tablespoons chestnut puree

1¼ cups (266 g) packed dark brown
sugar

1 cup (200 g) granulated sugar

3 large eggs, at room temperature

1½ cups (360 g) buttermilk

## FOR THE SALAM PAK SPICE CAKE

Preheat the oven to 350°F (180°C). Grease a 9 × 13-inch (23 × 33 cm) pan with butter or cooking spray.

In a medium bowl, whisk together the cake flour, baking soda, chai masala, ground ginger, mace, and salt until well combined.

In a stand mixer fitted with the paddle, beat the butter, chestnut puree, brown sugar, and granulated sugar on high speed for 7 minutes, scraping down the sides of the bowl as needed. Add the eggs one at a time, mixing well after each addition. Add the flour mixture in three additions, alternating with the buttermilk, beginning and ending with the flour, mixing on low speed after each addition. Pour the batter into the prepared baking pan.

Bake until a toothpick inserted in the center comes out clean, 30 to 35 minutes.

Let the cake cool in the pan for 15 minutes, then turn the cake out onto a wire rack to cool completely.

CONTINUED

## BROWN BUTTER SPICE FROSTING

2 sticks (226 g) unsalted butter, at room temperature

1 tablespoon whole milk powder

2 tablespoons heavy cream

2 teaspoons vanilla extract

1 teaspoon fresh lemon juice

½ teaspoon kosher salt

¼ teaspoon ground cinnamon

¼ teaspoon Chai Masala (page 24)

3¼ cups (368 g) powdered sugar

Gel food coloring

## FOR DECORATING

½ cup (54 g) pistachios, coarsely chopped

¼ cup (23 g) ground pistachios

¼ cup (27 g) slivered almonds

## FOR THE BROWN BUTTER SPICE FROSTING

In a saucepan, melt 1 stick (113 g) of the butter over medium heat and cook the butter until you start to see just a few brown specks of caramelized milk solids, 5 to 6 minutes. Add the milk powder and stir until all the milk solids and milk powder have browned and caramelized. Remove from the heat and cool completely.

In a stand mixer fitted with the paddle, combine the remaining 1 stick (113 g) of butter, the heavy cream, vanilla, lemon juice, salt, cinnamon, chai masala, and powdered sugar. Mix on low speed until combined and then mix on high speed until light and fluffy, about 3 minutes.

Measure out ¼ cup (50 g) of frosting and add food coloring and mix well. Spoon the frosting into a piping bag and snip off a small, thin hole. Spoon 2 tablespoons of plain white frosting into a piping bag and snip off a small, thin hole as well.

## TO DECORATE

Spread the rest of the frosting over the cake into an even layer using an offset spatula. Use a toothpick to draw out a 3 × 2-inch (7.5 × 5 cm) grid onto the cake. Fill each square with a pattern of chopped pistachios, ground pistachios, and almonds. Using the colored frosting and plain frosting in the piping bags, pipe lines down the top of the cake to mimic a line of stitches.

Refrigerate until ready to serve.

- - - - - - - - - - - - - - - - - - - - - - - - - - - - - - - - - - - - - - - - -

## MAKE IT SIMPLE

Dollop all the frosting onto the cake and spread it out into an even, fluffy layer using an offset spatula or the back of a large spoon. Sprinkle on the chopped pistachios and serve.

## MAKE IT EGGLESS

Use ½ cup (100 g) sour cream and ¼ cup (56 g) vegan mayonnaise in place of the eggs and add 1½ teaspoons of baking powder to the dry ingredients.

# MINI KAJU PISTA BURFI SWISS ROLL CAKES

No matter how hard my mom tried, she could not keep me and my sister's grubby little hands out of a box of pista burfis when we were little. Kaju pista burfi is a super popular mithai (sweet) that's given out during Diwali. It's pistachio fudge wrapped with cashew fudge and rolled into a log. They're typically decorated with shiny silver vark (foil) or silver leaf, which is what attracted us to them so much! I wanted to increase the scale of these tiny mithai into mini Swiss rolls (also called jelly rolls). Instead of decorating with silver vark, I used gold! The cake is surprisingly light, and the whipped cream filling is even lighter! It practically melts in your mouth. These would be so cute on a dessert table for Holi or Diwali!

MAKES 12 MINI SWISS ROLLS

## SPONGE CAKE

Softened butter, for the pan

4 large eggs, separated

½ cup (100 g) granulated sugar

2 tablespoons whole milk

2 tablespoons vegetable oil

4 tablespoons (60 g) unsalted butter, melted

1 teaspoon vanilla extract

½ cup (60 g) all-purpose flour

¼ cup (20 g) finely ground cashews

½ teaspoon kosher salt

## PISTACHIO WHIPPED CREAM

¾ cup (180 ml) heavy cream

½ teaspoon ground cardamom

¼ cup (28 g) powdered sugar

Green food coloring

¼ cup (23 g) ground pistachios

### FOR THE SPONGE CAKE

Preheat the oven to 350°F (180°C). Grease a 9 × 13-inch (23 × 33 cm) pan with butter and line with parchment paper.

In a medium bowl, whisk the egg whites until frothy. Gradually add ¼ cup (50 g) of the sugar and whip until stiff peaks. Set aside.

In a separate bowl, whisk the egg yolks with the remaining ¼ cup (50 g) of sugar. Add the milk, vegetable oil, melted butter, and vanilla and whisk until well combined. Sift in the flour and add in the ground cashews and salt. Gently fold the batter until well combined. Add one-third of the egg whites to the batter and mix well. Then gently fold in the rest of the egg whites until well combined. Pour the batter into the prepared pan. Smooth into an even layer with an offset spatula.

Bake until the cake is lightly golden and springs back when gently poked, 11 to 12 minutes.

Flip the cake out onto a rack to cool completely. Once the cake has cooled, remove the parchment paper and carefully cut the cake into 2 thin layers. Then cut each layer crosswise in half so that you have four 4½ × 6½-inch (11.5 × 16.5 cm) rectangles.

### FOR THE PISTACHIO WHIPPED CREAM

In a bowl, with an electric mixer, combine the heavy cream, cardamom, powdered sugar, and green food coloring. Whisk until you have stiff peaks, 4 to 5 minutes. Do not overmix this; otherwise, you will end up with butter! Fold the ground pistachios into the whipped cream.

Spread a thin layer of the pistachio whipped cream onto each rectangle of cake. With a long side facing you, roll a rectangle up into a log and wrap tightly in plastic wrap. Repeat for the remaining rectangles. Refrigerate the cake logs for 1 hour to set.

CONTINUED

## WHITE CHOCOLATE SHELL

10½ ounces (300 g) chopped white chocolate (about 1¾ cups)

1 tablespoon coconut oil

Gold leaf, for decorating

## FOR THE WHITE CHOCOLATE SHELL

In a microwave-safe bowl, combine the white chocolate and coconut oil and microwave in 15-second increments, mixing well after each, until the chocolate has melted. (Alternatively, if you don't have a microwave, bring a small pot of water to a boil and set a small heatproof bowl on top of the pot, making sure the bowl does not touch the water. Add the chocolate and coconut oil to the bowl and stir until melted.)

Line a baking sheet with parchment paper. Unwrap the cake logs and cut each log into 3 equal pieces. Dip the bottom of each mini Swiss roll in the melted chocolate and place on the lined pan and refrigerate until set.

Place the mini Swiss rolls on a wire rack set over a sheet pan. Pour the melted chocolate over the cakes so they are completely covered. Use an offset spatula to spread the chocolate as needed. Refrigerate the cakes for 5 to 10 minutes, or until the chocolate sets.

Use a fluffy brush like a blush brush to add gold leaf to the top of each Swiss roll and serve.

- - - - - - - - - - - - - - - - - - - - - - - - - - - - - - - - - - - - - - - - -

### MAKE IT SIMPLE

You can make one big Swiss roll instead of 12 mini ones. Once the cake is baked and is still hot, place a kitchen towel over the cake and roll it up starting from a long side. Give it a little squeeze. Unroll it and peel off the parchment paper and roll up in the cloth again. Cool for 2 hours. Unroll the cake and fill it with the pistachio whipped cream. Roll the cake up and refrigerate for 1 hour before pouring the melted chocolate over the top.

### MAKE IT EGGLESS

Replace the egg whites with ½ cup (105 g) of aquafaba and use ¼ cup (56 g) of silken tofu to replace the yolks.

# CARDAMOM VANILLA YOGURT BUNDT CAKE

Diwali is the festival of lights and colors, and nothing is more beautiful than seeing the contrast between the bright fireworks and sparklers and the starry night sky. I wanted to capture that visual in a cake, and this is what I came up with! A chocolate-covered Bundt cake dotted with gold leaf that is bursting with bright colors once you cut into it. The cake flavors are reminiscent of shrikhand, a yogurt-based dessert that's typically spiced with cardamom.

MAKES ONE 6-CUP (1.4 L)
BUNDT CAKE

## BUNDT CAKE

Softened butter and cooking spray for the pan

6 tablespoons (90 ml) whole milk

3 tablespoons (45 g) full-fat vanilla Greek yogurt

1 tablespoon vanilla extract

14 tablespoons (200 g) unsalted butter, at room temperature

¾ cup plus 2 tablespoons (178 g) granulated sugar

1¼ teaspoons baking powder

½ teaspoon ground cardamom

½ teaspoon kosher salt

3 large eggs

1¾ cups (210 g) all-purpose flour

Gel or liquid food coloring

## CHOCOLATE GLAZE

9 ounces (255 g) dark chocolate, chopped (1½ cups)

1 tablespoon coconut oil

Gold leaf, for decorating

## FOR THE BUNDT CAKE

Preheat the oven to 325°F (160°C). Generously grease a 6-cup (1.4 L) Bundt cake pan liberally with butter and then cooking spray. Double greasing the Bundt pan assures that your Bundt cake will slide out without getting stuck!

In large cup, whisk together the milk, yogurt, and vanilla. Set aside.

In a stand mixer fitted with the paddle, beat the butter, sugar, baking powder, cardamom, and salt. Mix on high speed for 3 minutes, scraping the bowl down halfway through. Add the eggs one at a time, mixing well after each addition. Add the flour in three additions, alternating with the milk/yogurt mixture, beginning and ending with the flour, mixing after each addition on low speed. Once the flour has been incorporated, divide the batter evenly among four bowls. Fold in your choice of food coloring into each of the bowls.

Spoon dollops of each colored dough into the Bundt pan. Tap the pan on the counter four or five times to get rid of any air bubbles.

Bake until a toothpick inserted in the center comes out clean, 45 to 50 minutes.

Let the cake cool in the pan for 10 minutes and then turn the cake out onto a wire rack to cool completely.

## FOR THE CHOCOLATE GLAZE

In a microwave-safe bowl, combine the chocolate and coconut oil and microwave in 15-second increments, stirring well after each, until the chocolate is melted. (Alternatively, if you don't have a microwave, bring a small pot of water to a boil and set a small heatproof bowl on top of the pot, making sure the bowl does not touch the water. Add the chocolate and coconut oil to the bowl and stir until melted.)

Place the cake on a wire rack set over a baking pan. Pour the melted chocolate glaze over the cooled cake, making sure to coat every part of the cake. Let the cake set for 1 hour before moving the cake to your serving platter and decorating with gold leaf.

## MAKE IT EGGLESS

In a bowl, whisk together ¾ cup (270 g) of granulated sugar, 2½ cups (300 g) of all-purpose flour, 2¼ teaspoons of baking powder, ½ teaspoon of salt, and ½ teaspoon of cardamom. Add 7 tablespoons (100 g) of melted butter, 1 cup (244 g) of whole milk, ¼ cup (56 g) of plain yogurt, and 1 tablespoon of vanilla extract. Split the batter up into four bowls and dye each batter your choice of color. Pour each color randomly into the Bundt pan, alternating colors, and bake per the recipe.

# MANGO ◈ MURABBA CAKE

This is a classic pound cake that's sweetened up with some Mango Murabba (page 27)—homemade jam. There is something about the golden, translucent, jewel-like mango jam contrasted against the white-and-brown pound cake that just brings me so much joy! It reminds me of jewels set in antique gold! You could serve this cake with tea or coffee or a fat dollop of whipped cream and freshly sliced mangoes for an easy dessert.

MAKES ONE 8 × 4-INCH
(20 × 10 CM) LOAF

## MANGO JAM CAKE

Softened butter, for the pan

2 cups (240 g) all-purpose flour

2 teaspoons baking powder

¾ teaspoon kosher salt

2 sticks (226 g) unsalted butter, at room temperature

1 cup (200 g) granulated sugar

4 large eggs, at room temperature

1 egg yolk, at room temperature

⅓ cup (80 g) Mango Murabba (page 27)

2 teaspoons vanilla extract

## MANGO JAM GLAZE

¼ cup (30 g) powdered sugar

3 ½ tablespoons (50 g) Mango Murabba (page 27)

1½ tablespoons hot water

Powdered sugar, for dusting

⅔ cup (160 g) Mango Murabba (page 27), for decorating

## FOR THE MANGO JAM CAKE

Preheat the oven to 325°F (160°C). Grease an 8 × 4-inch (20 × 10 cm) loaf pan with butter.

In a medium bowl, whisk together the flour, baking powder, and salt.

In a stand mixer fitted with the paddle, beat together the butter and granulated sugar on high speed for 3 minutes, scraping down the bowl halfway through. Add the whole eggs and egg yolk, one at a time, mixing well after each addition until just combined. Add the mango jam and vanilla and mix until combined. Add the flour mixture and mix on low speed until just combined.

Spoon the batter into the loaf pan and spread it into an even layer. Tap the pan on the counter four or five times.

Bake until a toothpick inserted in the center comes out clean, 50 minutes to 1 hour. The cake will be quite dark.

Let the cake cool in the pan for 10 minutes before turning it out onto a wire rack to cool slightly.

## WHILE THE CAKE IS WARM, MAKE THE JAM GLAZE

In a bowl, whisk together the powdered sugar, mango jam, and hot water until smooth. Brush the glaze onto the top and sides of the cake. Let the cake cool completely and dust with powdered sugar.

Spoon additional mango jam down the center of the top of the cake slices before serving. Store in an airtight container in the refrigerator for up to 4 days.

- - - - - - - - - - - - - - - - - - - - - - - - - - - - - - - - - - - - - - - - -

## MAKE IT EGGLESS

Use ½ cup (100 g) of sour cream, 6½ cups (100 g) of whole-milk Greek yogurt, and 1 tablespoon of vegan mayonnaise in place of the eggs and egg yolk and add an additional 1 teaspoon of baking powder to the flour mixture. The cake will have a tart flavor due to the yogurt and will take about 10 minutes longer to bake.

# ORANGE-PINEAPPLE CAKE

This summer I shared my family's ice cream spot in New Jersey, Applegate Farm, on my Instagram. Turns out my family wasn't the only one obsessed with their orange-pineapple ice cream! We always had a gallon tub of it in our freezer for when guests came over, especially around Diwali. I'm not sure what made this flavor so popular with desis in Jersey, but it is, and it's delicious! This cake is super fluffy, and the whipped cream topping makes it even lighter and gives it that creamy flavor and feel.

MAKES ONE 9-INCH (23 CM) CAKE

## ORANGE-PINEAPPLE CAKE

Softened butter, for the pan

1 egg white, at room temperature

1 cup plus 3 tablespoons (141 g) cake flour

1 ½ teaspoons baking powder

¼ teaspoon kosher salt

¾ cup (150 g) granulated sugar

1 tablespoon grated orange zest

4 tablespoons (56 g) unsalted butter, at room temperature

1 teaspoon vanilla extract

2 tablespoons orange juice

½ cup (123 g) crushed pineapple, fresh or canned

## TOPPING

1 cup (240 ml) heavy cream

¼ cup (28 g) powdered sugar, or to taste

1 teaspoon vanilla extract

Orange slices and edible flowers, for decoration

## FOR THE ORANGE-PINEAPPLE CAKE

Preheat the oven to 350°F (180°C). Line a 9-inch (23 cm) round cake pan with parchment paper and grease well with softened butter.

In a small bowl, with an electric mixer, beat the egg white on high until stiff peaks form. The whipped egg white should hold a peak when a whisk is dipped into it without flopping to the side. Set aside.

In a medium bowl, whisk together the flour, baking powder, and salt. Set aside.

In the bowl of a stand mixer, combine the granulated sugar and orange zest and use your fingers to rub the zest into the sugar until the sugar is pale orange. Snap on the paddle, add the butter, and mix at high speed for 4 minutes.

Add the vanilla, orange juice, and crushed pineapple and mix well for 1 minute. It might look curdled. That's okay—don't stress! Add the flour mixture and mix until it is just incorporated. Fold in the whipped egg whites until there are no streaks of white or yellow batter. Spoon the batter into the prepared pan and spread it into an even layer with a spatula.

Bake until a toothpick inserted into the center comes out clean, 25 to 30 minutes.

Let the cake cool in the pan for 10 minutes, then turn out onto a wire rack to cool completely.

## FOR THE TOPPING

In a bowl, whisk the heavy cream, powdered sugar, and vanilla until you reach stiff peaks, 4 to 5 minutes. Do not overmix this; otherwise, you will end up with butter! Spoon the whipped cream onto the cake and spread it over the entirety of the cake. Decorate with orange slices and edible flowers.

- - - - - - - - - - - - - - - - - - - - - - - - - - - - - - - - - - - - -

## MAKE IT EGGLESS

Use 3 tablespoons (40 g) of concentrated aquafaba (page 15) in place of the egg whites and whip as directed.

# COCONUT BURFI BUNDT CAKE

This Bundt cake is inspired by the flavors of coconut burfi, a coconut and cardamom fudge. It's a basic pound cake that's zhuzhed up with a little cardamom and full-fat coconut milk and then glazed with a sweet coconut glaze. Make sure to use coconut milk that does not have any preservatives or thickeners as they can have an aftertaste.

MAKES ONE 6-CUP (1.4 L) BUNDT CAKE OR 6 MINI BUNDT CAKES

## COCONUT CARDAMOM BUNDT CAKE

Softened butter and cooking spray, for the pan(s)

2¾ cups (330 g) all-purpose flour

4 teaspoons baking powder

½ teaspoon ground cardamom

¼ teaspoon kosher salt

1½ sticks (170 g) unsalted butter, at room temperature

1¾ cups (350 g) granulated sugar

4 large eggs, at room temperature

1 teaspoon vanilla extract

1 cup (240 ml) canned full-fat coconut milk

## COCONUT GLAZE

¼ cup (60 ml) canned full-fat coconut milk

1½ cups (170 g) powdered sugar

½ teaspoon vanilla extract

Pinch of ground cardamom

2 tablespoons unsweetened shredded coconut, toasted

## FOR THE COCONUT CARDAMOM BUNDT CAKE

Preheat the oven to 350°F (180°C). Generously grease a 6-cup (1.4 L) Bundt cake pan or 6 mini Bundt cake pans with butter and spray with cooking spray. Double greasing the Bundt pan assures that your Bundt cake will slide out without getting stuck!

In a medium bowl, whisk together the flour, baking powder, cardamom, and salt.

In a bowl, with an electric mixer, cream the butter and granulated sugar together until pale and fluffy, about 3 minutes. Add the eggs one at a time, mixing well after each addition. Add the vanilla and mix for 1 minute. Add the flour mixture in three additions, alternating with the coconut milk, beginning and ending with the flour, mixing well after each addition. Spoon the batter into the prepared Bundt cake pan(s). Gently tap the pan(s) on the counter to get rid of any air bubbles.

Bake until a toothpick inserted in the center comes out clean, 35 to 40 minutes for the large cake or 20 to 25 minutes for the mini Bundts.

Let cool for 10 minutes in the pan, then flip the cake(s) out onto a serving plate and give it a gentle tap on the counter to help dislodge the cake if needed. Let the cake(s) cool completely.

## FOR THE COCONUT GLAZE

In a small bowl, whisk together the coconut milk, powdered sugar, vanilla, and cardamom until smooth. Spoon the glaze over the cake and gently nudge the frosting over the edges using a spoon. Sprinkle with toasted coconut and serve.

- - - - - - - - - - - - - - - - - - - - - - - - - - - - -

### MAKE IT EGGLESS

Use ½ cup (100 g) of sour cream and 6½ cups (100 g) of whole-milk Greek yogurt in place of the eggs and add an additional 1 teaspoon of baking powder to the flour mixture.

# SHRIKHAND YOGURT CAKE

I don't know about you guys, but my house ALWAYS had leftover shrikhand (a lightly sweetened, thick yogurt dessert that's spiced with cardamom and saffron) in the fridge after a big family dinner, especially after Diwali. We'd just eat it with dinner throughout the week or try and pawn it off on guests or family members who might have the (mis)fortune of visiting us after a jamvanu (dinner party). Well, if you're like my family, here is a great way to use up some of that leftover shrikhand taking up space in your fridge! This French-style yogurt cake is super simple to make and is eggless! I drizzled a quick icing on it that was also made with leftover shrikhand to give it that extra yogurty tang. Because the cake is eggless, it's extremely delicate, so be gentle when unmolding it from the pan!

MAKES 6 MINI BUNDT CAKES OR ONE
6-CUP (1.4 L) BUNDT CAKE

## YOGURT CAKE

Softened butter and cooking spray,
for the pans

1½ cups (180 g) all-purpose flour

1 tablespoon baking powder

¼ teaspoon kosher salt

1¼ cups (300 g) shrikhand
(see Notes)

½ cup (100 g) granulated sugar

½ teaspoon vanilla extract

½ teaspoon ground cardamom

½ cup (110 g) vegetable oil

¼ cup (60 ml) whole milk,
at room temperature

## GLAZE

1 tablespoon shrikhand

1½ tablespoons milk

1 cup (113 g) powdered sugar

2 tablespoons chopped pistachios

### FOR THE YOGURT CAKE

Preheat the oven to 350°F (180°C). Grease 6 mini Bundt pans or one 6-cup (1.4 L) Bundt pan liberally with butter and then cooking spray. Double greasing the Bundt pan assures that your Bundt cake will slide out without getting stuck!

In a small bowl, whisk together the flour, baking powder, and salt until well combined.

In a large bowl, whisk together the shrikhand, granulated sugar, vanilla, ground cardamom, oil, and milk until well combined. Gently fold in the flour mixture until there are no clumps of dry flour. The batter will be slightly thick. Spoon the batter into the prepared pan(s) and use a spoon or spatula to spread the batter into an even layer. Tap the pan(s) on the counter five or six times to get rid of any air bubbles.

Bake until a toothpick inserted into the center of a cake comes out clean, 18 to 20 minutes for the mini Bundts or 25 to 35 minutes for the large cake.

Let the cake(s) cool in the pan(s) for 10 minutes, then turn the cake(s) out onto a wire rack to cool completely.

### MAKE THE GLAZE

In a small bowl, whisk together the shrikhand, milk, and powdered sugar until you have a thick, smooth icing that runs slowly off your whisk. Spoon the icing onto the completely cooled cake(s) and gently spread it out. Top with chopped pistachios and enjoy!

### NOTES

- You can also bake this cake in an 8 × 4-inch (20 × 10 cm) loaf pan or a 9-inch (23 cm) round cake pan. The baking times will be 25 to 35 minutes for the loaf pan and 20 to 25 minutes for the cake pan.

- If you don't have leftover shrikhand, use 1¼ cups (300 g) of whole milk Greek yogurt mixed with a small pinch of saffron and ½ teaspoon of ground cardamom.

# VANILLA & ROSE PETIT CAKES

I know these cakes look complicated or like they'll take forever to make—but they won't. I promise! The cakes take just a few minutes to bake, and they are absolutely adorable to look at! It's a simple vanilla sponge topped with vanilla and cardamom whipped cream and strawberry rose jam in the center. You can swap out the strawberry rose filling for Mango Murabba (page 27) or Pear & Cardamom Jam (page 28).

MAKES 6 MINI CAKES

## SPONGE CAKE

Softened butter, for the pan

4 egg whites (132 g total)

Pinch of kosher salt

¼ teaspoon cream of tartar

Pink food coloring (optional)

¼ cup (50 g) granulated sugar

4 egg yolks (68 g total)

3½ tablespoons (50 g) unsalted butter, melted

1 teaspoon vanilla extract

⅓ cup (40 g) all-purpose flour

## STRAWBERRY ROSE FILLING

3 tablespoons (66 g) strawberry jam

⅛ teaspoon rose water, store-bought or homemade (page 23)

## CARDAMOM VANILLA WHIPPED CREAM

½ cup (120 ml) heavy cream

¼ teaspoon ground cardamom

½ teaspoon vanilla extract

¼ cup (28 g) powdered sugar

## FOR DECORATING (OPTIONAL)

Chopped pistachios

Dried edible flower petals

### FOR THE SPONGE CAKE

Preheat the oven to 350°F (180°C). Grease a 9 × 13-inch (23 × 33 cm) pan with butter and line with parchment paper.

In a large bowl, with an electric mixer, whisk the egg whites with the salt and cream of tartar until frothy. Add food coloring if using. Gradually add 2 tablespoons of the granulated sugar and whip until stiff peaks form. Set aside.

In a separate bowl, whisk the egg yolks with the remaining 2 tablespoons of sugar. Slowly stream in the melted butter. Whisk in the vanilla. Mix until well incorporated. Sift in the flour and whisk until just combined. Add one-third of the whipped egg whites to the batter and whisk well. Then gently fold in the rest of the egg whites until well combined. Pour the batter into the prepared baking pan and gently smooth the batter out into a thin, even layer. Remember this is a thin cake!

Bake until the cake is set and the top springs back when gently poked, about 11 minutes.

While the cake is hot, flip it out onto a wire rack and peel off the parchment paper. Cool completely.

### FOR THE STRAWBERRY ROSE FILLING

In a small bowl, whisk together the strawberry jam and rose water until well combined. Spoon the mixture into a piping bag or sandwich bag with a small corner snipped off and set aside.

### FOR THE CARDAMOM VANILLA WHIPPED CREAM

In a separate bowl, with an electric mixer, whip the heavy cream, cardamom, vanilla, and powdered sugar until you reach stiff peaks, 4 to 5 minutes. Do not overmix this; otherwise, you will end up with butter! Spoon the whipped cream into a piping bag fitted with a small round tip or large sandwich bag with ¼ inch (6 mm) snipped off one corner.

CONTINUED

Use a 2-inch (5 cm) round cookie cutter to punch out small rounds from the sheet of cake, to get a total of 18 rounds. Take 6 cake rounds and pipe small dollops of whipped cream around the edge of each cake. Pipe about ½ teaspoon of strawberry filling onto the center of the cake. Top with another cake round and repeat piping the whipped cream and strawberry filling. Once you've added a third and final cake layer, use a large star tip to pipe a dollop of whipped cream on top.

## TO DECORATE

If desired, sprinkle with some chopped pistachios and edible flower petals. Enjoy within a few hours.

- - - - - - - - - - - - - - - - - - - - - - - - - - - - - - - - - - - - - - - - - - - - - - - -

## MAKE IT EGGLESS

Use ⅔ cup (132 g) concentrated aquafaba (page 15) in place of the egg white and whip as directed. Use ¼ cup (54 g) silken tofu in place of the egg yolk.

# MUD WORK CAKE

This cake is inspired by mud work, also known as lippan art or mirror work. It's an art form that is found in Gujarat, specifically in Kutch. It's made by molding ropes and dots of clay in a geometric pattern around small mirrors. This art form is used to decorate the inside walls of homes, sometimes applied directly onto the walls or onto canvases. Typically, it's done in all white, but you can also find multicolored mud work, too. My mom had two or three pieces of mud work art that she displayed in our home when I was growing up, and I remember loving how the sun would reflect off of them in the afternoon light. This a chocolate sheet cake recipe with a salted vanilla Swiss meringue buttercream frosting. I used various shapes of silver dragées to mimic the mirrors.

MAKES ONE 8-INCH (20 CM)
SQUARE CAKE

## CHOCOLATE CAKE

Cooking spray or softened butter, for the pan

¾ cup (180 ml) whole milk

6 tablespoons (85 g) unsalted butter

1 ounce (30 g) dark chocolate, finely chopped (about 3 tablespoons)

3 tablespoons (17 g) unsweetened cocoa powder

¼ teaspoon instant coffee (optional)

½ teaspoon kosher salt

½ cup (100 g) granulated sugar

½ cup (107 g) packed dark brown sugar

1 large egg

1 teaspoon vanilla extract

1 cup (120 g) all-purpose flour

## SALTED VANILLA SWISS MERINGUE FROSTING

⅓ cup (85 g) egg whites

½ cup (100 g) granulated sugar

⅛ teaspoon cream of tartar

½ teaspoon kosher salt

9 tablespoons (1278 g) unsalted butter, at room temperature

½ cup (60 g) powdered sugar

1 teaspoon vanilla extract

### FOR THE CHOCOLATE CAKE

Preheat the oven to 350°F (180°C). Grease an 8-inch (20 cm) square pan with cooking spray or butter.

In a large saucepan, combine the milk and butter and cook over medium heat until the butter is melted. Remove from the heat and add the dark chocolate, unsweetened cocoa powder, instant coffee (if using), and salt. Whisk until smooth. Add the granulated sugar and brown sugar and whisk for 2 minutes. Add the egg and vanilla and whisk until well combined. Sift in the flour and mix until the flour is just incorporated and there are no lumps. Pour the batter into the prepared baking pan.

Bake until a toothpick inserted in the center comes out clean, 20 to 23 minutes.

Let the cake cool in the pan for 10 minutes, then flip the cake out onto a wire rack to cool completely.

### FOR THE SALTED VANILLA SWISS MERINGUE FROSTING

Meanwhile, in the bowl of a stand mixer, combine the egg whites, granulated sugar, cream of tartar, and salt. Bring a pot (that can hold the mixer bowl) of water to a simmer. Set the bowl over the pot, making sure the bottom of the bowl doesn't touch the water. Stir for 5 minutes, or until the mixture hits 160°F (71°C). Remove the bowl from the pan.

Set the bowl on the mixer and snap on the whisk. Whisk for 12 minutes. Add the butter a tablespoon at a time, mixing well after each addition. Add the powdered sugar and vanilla. Scrape down the bowl and whisk well. If it's soupy or loose, pop the bowl in the fridge for 15 minutes and then continue whisking. It should be creamy, smooth, and light. Spoon one-quarter of the buttercream into a piping bag fitted with a medium round tip (Ateco 803).

CONTINUED

**FOR DECORATING**

Silver dragées, in multiple shapes

**TO DECORATE**

Spread a thin layer of frosting on the top and sides of the chocolate cake. This is the crumb coat, which traps the crumbs on the cake so that they don't mess up your cake as you continue frosting. Freeze the cake for 15 minutes.

Spread the rest of the frosting over the top and sides of the cake using an offset spatula. Smooth the top of the cake so that it's nice and smooth and level. Use various large cookie cutters to gently and lightly press a pattern on top of the cake. I used a large flower cookie cutter and round cookie cutter. Then use the lines as a guide and pipe the frosting on top of the lines. Press silver dragées into the cake to create a geometric pattern. Serve immediately or refrigerate for up to 2 days. When ready to serve, let the cake sit until it comes to room temperature before slicing.

**MAKE IT SIMPLE**

If you want to decorate this cake simply, skip the buttercream line work and just frost the cake and place the dragées on the cake in a geometric pattern.

**MAKE IT EGGLESS**

In the cake batter, use ¼ cup (50 g) of sour cream in place of the egg. For the frosting, use ⅓ cup (7 g) of concentrated aquafaba (page 15) in place of the egg whites. You do not need to heat up the aquafaba; instead, skip directly to whipping the aquafaba with the cream of tartar, sugar, and salt until it's fluffy. Fold in the butter per the recipe.

# ORANGE FENNEL VANILLA CUPCAKES

The first time I had orange and fennel together, it was at Malai, an Indian-inspired ice cream shop in New York City. Pooja, the creator of Malai, blew my mind with this flavor! I took inspiration from her combo to make these cupcakes decorated like Rabari embroidery.

Rabari embroidery (pictured on page 165) is done in the Kutch part of Gujarat. This style of embroidery is usually done with bright and colorful threads that are chain stitched, and occasionally mirrors are added in. My mom has been doing this type of embroidery for ages and taught me simple motifs I could embroider onto my dresses. You'll find this type of embroidery on traditional Chaniya cholis (Gujarati folk wear), pillowcases, wall hangings, purses, and more. It's time-consuming and requires a lot of patience. My mother made hand-embroidered curtains with over fifty mirrors for my daughter using Rabari embroidering techniques. It took her over twenty hours total to do! Luckily these cupcakes won't take that long!

MAKES 12 CUPCAKES

### ORANGE FENNEL CUPCAKES

1⅓ cups (160 g) all-purpose flour

2¼ teaspoons baking powder

¼ teaspoon kosher salt

¼ teaspoon freshly ground fennel seeds

¾ cup (150 g) granulated sugar

2 teaspoons grated orange zest

6 tablespoons (85 g) unsalted butter, at room temperature

1 large egg, at room temperature

1 egg white, at room temperature

1½ teaspoons vanilla extract

¾ cup (180 g) whole milk

### VANILLA BUTTERCREAM

2 sticks (226 g) unsalted butter, at room temperature

4 cups (450 g) powdered sugar

1 tablespoon milk

2 teaspoons vanilla extract

⅛ teaspoon almond extract

⅛ teaspoon kosher salt

### FOR THE ORANGE FENNEL CUPCAKES

Preheat the oven to 375°F (190°C). Line 12 cups of a muffin tin with paper liners.

In a medium bowl, whisk together the flour, baking powder, salt, and fennel until well combined.

In a bowl of a stand mixer, combine the granulated sugar and orange zest and use your fingers to rub the zest into the sugar until it's pale orange. Snap on the paddle, add the butter, and mix for 6 minutes, scraping the bowl down halfway through. Add the whole egg, egg white, and vanilla and mix for another minute. Add the flour mixture in three additions, alternating with the milk, beginning and ending with the flour and scraping down the bowl as needed. Divide the batter among the lined muffin cups, filling each cup three-quarters full.

Bake until a toothpick inserted in the center of a cupcake comes out clean, 15 to 18 minutes.

Let the cupcakes cool in the pan.

### FOR THE VANILLA BUTTERCREAM

Meanwhile, in a stand mixer fitted with the paddle, beat the butter, powdered sugar, milk, vanilla, almond extract, and salt on medium speed until the frosting is fluffy and pale, 4 to 5 minutes. Spoon the frosting into a large piping bag fitted with a large round tip (Ateco 808).

CONTINUED

## FOR DECORATING

Gel food coloring

Dragées or sprinkles

## TO DECORATE

Line a baking sheet with parchment paper. Pipe a large dollop of frosting onto the top of each cupcake. Flip the cupcakes upside down and gently press the top of each cupcake onto the parchment paper to make a flat top. Leave them upside down and freeze the tray of cupcakes for 15 minutes. Gently peel the cupcakes off the parchment paper.

Take any leftover frosting and split it into three or four bowls and color each frosting with food coloring of your choice. Spoon each color into a piping bag fitted with small round tip (Ateco 4) or small star tip (Ateco 13). Pipe various stitches onto each cupcake using the colored frosting. See below for some piping ideas.

If you mess up, just freeze the cupcake for 10 minutes and use a table knife to scrape off the mistake!

Serve immediately or refrigerate for 4 to 6 days in an airtight container.

- - - - - - - - - - - - - - - - - - - - - - - - - - - - - - - - - - - - - - - - -

## MAKE IT EGGLESS

Use 3 tablespoons (42 g) of vegan mayonnaise in place of the whole egg and ⅓ cup (70 g) of concentrated aquafaba (page 15) in place of the egg white. Add ¼ teaspoon of baking soda to the dry ingredients.

# PINEAPPLE CREAM CAKE

When I went to India earlier this year, I noticed that almost every bakery had cream cakes in their windows, pineapple being one of the most popular fillings! The tart pineapple and light fluffy whipped cream just work well together. If you have a family member who loves getting fruit-filled cakes for their birthday, this is the cake to make! I cut the whipped cream with mascarpone cream to help stabilize it (see Note). I used fresh pineapple for this cake, but, if you use canned, be sure to drain the pineapple well before using.

My inspiration for the cake design was floral rangoli. Rangoli is an art form that is typically done on the floors of homes. They can be made from rice, colored powders, paint, and flowers. The shapes are geometrical and symmetrical, similar to mandala. You'll see rangoli with tea lights dotted throughout the designs in people's homes during Diwali and Holi. I used marigold flower petals to create my design, but you can use nuts or sprinkles as well. To make it simpler, you can dot marigold petals randomly over the cake or place whole flowers over the cake top.

MAKES ONE 9-INCH (23 CM)
TWO-LAYER CAKE

## CAKE

Cooking spray, for the pans

10 tablespoons (143 g) unsalted butter, at room temperature

1¼ cups (250 g) granulated sugar

2½ teaspoons baking powder

½ teaspoon kosher salt

⅓ cup (89 g) egg whites

1¼ teaspoons vanilla extract

1¾ cups plus 3 tablespoons (229 g) cake flour

¾ cup plus 2 tablespoons (216 g) whole milk

## VANILLA MASCARPONE WHIPPED CREAM

1½ cups (340 g) heavy cream, cold

8 ounces (225 g) mascarpone cheese, cold

1 cup (113 g) powdered sugar

1 tablespoon whole milk

### FOR THE CAKE

Preheat the oven to 350°F (180°C). Grease two 9-inch (23 cm) round cake pans with cooking spray and line with parchment paper.

In a stand mixer fitted with the paddle, beat the butter, granulated sugar, baking powder, and salt on high speed for 7 minutes, scraping down the bowl halfway through. Add the egg whites and vanilla and mix for 1 minute. Add the flour in three additions, alternating with the milk, beginning and ending with the flour, scraping down the sides after each addition.

Divide the batter (about 463 g per pan) between the two prepared baking pans. Use a spatula to spread the batter into an even layer and tap the pans on the counter four or five times to get rid of any air bubbles.

Bake until a toothpick inserted in the center comes out clean, 20 to 22 minutes.

Let the cakes cool in the pans for 10 minutes before turning them out onto a wire rack to cool completely.

### FOR THE VANILLA MASCARPONE WHIPPED CREAM

Meanwhile, in a stand mixer fitted with the whisk, beat the heavy cream, mascarpone, powdered sugar, and milk on low speed for 2 minutes. Increase the speed to medium-high and whisk until you have stiff peaks. Do not overmix the frosting as it'll split! Spoon half the whipped cream into a piping bag fitted with a large round tip. Refrigerate the mascarpone whipped cream until ready to use.

CONTINUED

## ASSEMBLY

¾ cup (120 g) finely chopped fresh pineapple

Edible flower petals, such as marigolds, calendula, roses, etc.

## TO ASSEMBLE

Place a tablespoon of the mascarpone whipped cream onto a cake board and place one layer of cake on top. Spread about ½ cup (120 g) of whipped cream on top of the cake into a thin even layer. Pipe a circle of frosting around the edge of the cake. This will act as a wall so that your pineapple filling doesn't squish out! Spoon the chopped pineapple into the center of the cake and spread it into an even layer. Add ½ cup (120 g) of whipped cream on top of the pineapple and gently spread the whipped cream into an even layer. Place the second layer of cake on top, making sure it's level and evenly placed. Pipe whipped cream into the crack between the two cake layers—it's okay if you have a little excess coming out! Using an offset spatula, scrape away any excess whipped cream and frost the top and sides of the cake with a thin layer of whipped cream to make the crumb coat. Chill the cake for 30 minutes in the fridge.

Use the remaining whipped cream to frost the rest of the cake. I like to use a bench scraper while turning the cake to make smooth sides and then use an offset spatula to even out the top of the cake. Use edible flower petals to create a rangoli-style design on top.

---

### SWITCH IT UP

Feel free to add ¼ teaspoon of ground cardamom to the mascarpone whipped cream for a more desi flavor.

### MAKE IT EGGLESS

Use 6 tablespoons (89 g) of concentrated aquafaba (page 15) in place of the egg whites and add ½ teaspoon of baking soda and an additional ½ teaspoon of baking powder to the butter before creaming. Use the same weight of all-purpose flour to replace the cake flour. The cake will be delicate, so be sure to handle it carefully.

### NOTE

- If you were to frost the cake with whipped cream alone, the cream would deflate over time and not hold. Adding mascarpone helps stabilize the whipped cream without having to add things like gelatin to it!

# Tarts & Pies

# CHOCOLATE, FIG & STAR ANISE CRÉMEUX TART

If you need a showstopper for your holiday party, trust me, this is it! This tart has a buttery star anise shortbread crust filled with a rich decadent dark chocolate crémeux topped with tons of fresh figs and dollops of whipped cream. Crémeux is a cross between a ganache and mousse and is smooth and creamy in texture. Think of it as a fancy chocolate ganache tart!

The design was inspired by a dye-resistant block printing technique called ajrakh. It's done by block printing fabric using lime and gum arabic, which are dye resistant, and then dying the fabric, typically with natural dyes. The result is a design created by the negative space that is created by the dye-resistant pattern.

MAKES ONE 9-INCH (23 CM) TART

## ANISE SHORTBREAD CRUST

½ cup (60 g) all-purpose flour

⅔ cup (57 g) almond flour

⅓ cup (57 g) white rice flour

⅓ cup (60 g) granulated sugar

½ teaspoon kosher salt

½ teaspoon ground star anise

4 tablespoons (57 g) unsalted butter, at room temperature

## DARK CHOCOLATE CRÉMEUX

⅓ cup (80 ml) whole milk

⅔ cup (160 ml) heavy cream

2 large eggs

2½ tablespoons (31 g) granulated sugar

10.5 ounces (300 g) dark chocolate (70% cacao), chopped (1¾ cups)

### FOR THE ANISE SHORTBREAD CRUST

Preheat the oven to 350°F (180°C).

In a small bowl, whisk together the all-purpose flour, almond meal, rice flour, sugar, salt, and anise. Add the butter and use your hands to rub the butter into the flour mixture until it has a coarse, sandy texture. Pour the mixture into a 9-inch (23 cm) tart pan or cake pan and use your hands or a measuring cup to press the mixture into an even layer on the bottom and sides of the pan. Dock the dough with a fork.

Bake until it is golden brown, 20 to 25 minutes. Let cool completely before filling.

### FOR THE DARK CHOCOLATE CRÉMEUX

In a saucepan, bring the milk and cream to a simmer and remove from the heat.

In a bowl, with an electric mixer, whisk together the eggs and granulated sugar on high speed until pale and fluffy, about 4 minutes. Slowly drizzle ½ cup (120 ml) of the warm milk mixture into the eggs while whisking. Once combined, add the warmed egg mixture to the saucepan with the rest of the milk mixture. Stir over medium heat until the mixture coats the back of a spoon and the custard reaches 82°F (28°C), 4 to 5 minutes.

Pour the custard into a heatproof bowl and add the chocolate. Let the mixture sit for 1 minute before whisking to a smooth glossy chocolate crémeux. If the mixture looks broken, use an immersion blender to blend the chocolate until it's smooth. Let the crémeux cool for 15 minutes. Pour it into the cooled tart shell and use an offset spatula to smooth it into a nice even layer. Cover with plastic wrap and

CONTINUED

**FOR DECORATING**

¼ cup (60 ml) heavy cream

1 tablespoon powdered sugar

½ teaspoon vanilla extract

3 to 4 fresh figs, 2 thinly sliced crosswise and 2 quartered

refrigerate for at least 4 hours or overnight. The tart can be stored in the fridge for up to 4 days at this point. Hold off on making the whipped cream and decorating the tart until ready to serve.

**FOR DECORATING**

In a small bowl, with an electric mixer, whisk the heavy cream, powdered sugar, and vanilla until you have stiff peaks, for 4 to 5 minutes. Don't overmix it as it'll turn into butter! Spoon the whipped cream into a piping bag fitted with a small round tip. Remove the tart from the fridge and arrange the sliced fig on the tart to create a symmetrical shape/design. Pipe dollops of whipped cream on top and arrange the quartered figs on top, using the whipped cream to help secure the figs onto the tart. Serve immediately or store in the fridge for up to 1 day.

**MAKE IT SIMPLE**

If you want to do a simple design, you can pipe dollops of whipped cream along the perimeter of the tart and then place quartered figs on top.

**MAKE IT EGGLESS**

Make a ganache instead of the crémeux by heating up 1½ cups (350 g) of heavy cream until it simmers and then pouring it over 2⅓ cups (350 g) of chopped dark chocolate. Whisk until smooth, pour it into the crust, and refrigerate until set (no need to cover in plastic wrap).

# KHEER TART

This tart is inspired by French riz au lait tarts, or rice pudding tarts. While riz au lait is spiced with vanilla or often orange zest, Indian rice pudding, or kheer, is spiced with saffron and cardamom. It can be served cold or warm, and it's usually served at big family get-together or at temples on religious holidays. My kheer is not too sweet, so feel free to add additional sugar if you'd like!

MAKES ONE 9-INCH (23 CM) TART

Sweet Tart Dough (page 32)

⅔ cup (112 g) basmati rice

1 tablespoon (15 g) unsalted butter

2 cups (480 ml) whole milk

¼ cup (50 g) granulated sugar

½ teaspoon ground cardamom

¼ teaspoon kosher salt

15 to 17 saffron threads

¼ cup (23 g) ground pistachios (optional)

Dried rose petals (optional)

Preheat the oven to 375°F (190°C).

Use your hands to press the tart dough into a 9-inch (23 cm) tart pan. Make sure to press the dough evenly up the sides and bottom of the pan. Dock the bottom and sides of the tart dough with a fork and freeze for 30 minutes or overnight.

Line the crust with parchment paper or foil and fill the crust with beans or pie weights. Bake the crust until the edges are lightly golden brown, 14 to 15 minutes. Remove the weights and liner and bake until the tart shell is golden brown, an additional 10 to 15 minutes. Let the tart shell cool.

Rinse the rice until the water runs clear and soak the rice in cold water for 30 minutes. Drain the rice and set aside.

In a medium saucepan, combine the butter and milk and bring to a boil over medium-high heat. Once the milk starts to boil, add the rice, sugar, cardamom, and salt and stir well. Simmer over low heat, stirring occasionally, until the rice is tender and soft, about 15 minutes. Remove the kheer from the heat and stir in the saffron. Let the kheer cool completely.

Spoon the kheer into the baked tart shell and spread it into an even layer. If desired, sprinkle the outside edge with pistachios and dried rose petals. Serve within 4 hours of making; otherwise, the crust will get soggy.

# APPLE CHAR-PIE

When I auditioned for *MasterChef*, this Indian-spiced apple pie filling is what got me my apron! The lattice work on my apple pie is inspired by the lattice work done on charpai, or Indian cots. Charpai (meaning "four-footed") are woven benches and cots that have brightly colored ropes or belts that are artfully woven together over a wooden frame. In India, my family sleeps on charpai that are topped with thick quilts called dhadkis.

For the apples, I like to use a mix of Granny Smith and Honeycrisp apples, but any mix of baking apples will work well! To make this eggless, you can use heavy cream instead of egg for the wash but keep in mind that the pie won't brown as deeply.

MAKES ONE 9-INCH (23 CM) PIE

Double recipe Pie Dough (page 32), for 2 crusts

4 pounds (1.8 kg) apples, peeled, cored, and cut into ¼-inch (6 mm) slices

¼ cup (28 g) cornstarch

½ cup (100 g) granulated sugar

½ cup (107 g) packed dark brown sugar or grated jaggery

1 tablespoon fresh lemon juice

2 teaspoons ground cinnamon

1 teaspoon ground cardamom

¾ teaspoon ground ginger

¼ teaspoon ground cloves

¼ teaspoon ground nutmeg

1½ teaspoons kosher salt

Liquid white food coloring

Liquid food coloring of your choice

1 large egg, beaten

Roll out one piece of the pie dough into a 12-inch (30 cm) round. Gently place the rolled-out pie dough into a 9-inch (23 cm) pie pan.

In a large bowl, combine the sliced apples, cornstarch, granulated sugar, brown sugar, lemon juice, cinnamon, cardamom, ginger, cloves, nutmeg, and salt. Gently mix until the apples are well coated. Lay the apple slices out in the pie shell so that all the slices are flat and stacked on top of each other. Pour in any juices that might be in the bowl.

To make the lattice, roll out the second piece of pie dough into a 12-inch (30 cm) round. Cut the dough into strips ½ inch (1.3 cm) wide. Gently place a few strips of the pie dough vertically over the pie, leaving a ½-inch (1.3 cm) gap in between them. Lift every third strip up and place a strip of pie dough horizontally (perpendicular to the strips on the pie) stretching across the top of the pie. Return the vertical strips back down over the dough. Count the third strip from the previously lifted strip of dough and lift that one up and repeat. Repeat until the whole pie has been latticed. Cut off any excess dough and use your knuckles and thumb to crimp the edges of the pie crust. Freeze the pie for 1 hour.

Preheat the oven to 400°F (200°C).

In each of two small containers, add 2 to 3 drops of liquid white food coloring. Add your choice of colors to each container and mix well. Brush the vertical strips of dough with one color and the horizontal strips with the second color. Freeze the pie again for 10 minutes. Brush the pie with the beaten egg. Bake until the crust is golden brown and the filling is bubbling, 1 hour 5 minutes to 1 hour 15 minutes. If the pie crust starts to get too brown, cover with foil and continue baking.

Let the pie cool for 30 minutes before serving.

## MAKE IT SIMPLE

Skip the charpai lattice weave and opt for a traditional lattice or just cover with a sheet of pie dough, crimp the edges to seal the pie, and cut 3 or 4 slits in the center of the pie to help vent the pie while it bakes.

# TENDER COCONUT CREAM PIE

I am 10,000 percent convinced that this recipe will the breakout star of this book. In India I had tender coconut ice cream from Naturals, a famous Indian ice cream franchise, and I will never be the same. It had chunks of soft tender coconut in it that gave it a rich texture. The tender coconut filling requires a bit of work since it's made with fresh young coconuts, but it's necessary to get that fresh tender coconut flavor! You can usually find young coconuts at the grocery store in the fresh produce section. This recipe ended up being my husband Rhut's favorite, and I've made it no less than fifteen times in the last few months!

I decorated the pie with colored shredded coconut to mimic the sunset over the salt flats and mountains at Kalo Dungar, in Kutch Gujarat. I highly recommend using Thai Kitchen's full-fat coconut milk in a carton instead of canned coconut milk, as it has a fresher taste and does not contain any thickeners or preservatives.

MAKES ONE 9-INCH (23 CM) PIE

## GRAHAM CRACKER CRUST

2 cups (200 g) graham cracker crumbs

¼ cup (50 g) granulated sugar

¼ teaspoon kosher salt

5 tablespoons (71 g) unsalted butter, melted

## TENDER COCONUT FILLING

1 young coconut

1¼ cups (300 ml) full-fat coconut milk

⅓ cup (60 g) granulated sugar

¼ cup (28 g) cornstarch

1 teaspoon vanilla extract

¼ teaspoon freshly ground cardamom

⅛ teaspoon kosher salt

### FOR THE GRAHAM CRACKER CRUST

Preheat the oven to 350°F (180°C).

In a small bowl, whisk together the graham cracker crumbs, granulated sugar, and salt. Add the melted butter and mix until you have a wet sand-like texture. Pour the crumbs into a 9-inch (23 cm) pie plate and use your hands or a flat-bottomed measuring cup to press the crumbs into the sides and bottom of the pie plate.

Bake the crust for 8 minutes to set. Let cool completely before filling.

### FOR THE TENDER COCONUT FILLING

Use a sharp chef's knife to shave off the top of the coconut until you see the lines on the hard shell of the coconut. Use the heel of the knife to hit a circle around the top of the exposed coconut. Peel the top part off and strain the coconut water into a cup. Use a spoon to scoop out the tender coconut meat for the pie. Be sure to wash off any hard bits of the coconut shell from the tender coconut meat!

In a blender, combine the coconut milk, ¼ cup (60 ml) coconut water, granulated sugar, cornstarch, ¼ cup (53 g) of the tender coconut, the vanilla, cardamom, and salt. Blend until smooth.

Pour the mixture into a saucepan and cook over high heat, stirring constantly, until the mixture thickens, 6 to 8 minutes. Once the custard gets thick, cook for another 2 minutes. Pour the custard onto a large plate and cover with plastic wrap. Freeze the custard for 30 minutes, or until cool.

CONTINUED

## WHIPPED CREAM

1⅓ cups (320 g) heavy cream

½ cup (60 g) powdered sugar

1 teaspoon vanilla extract

## SHREDDED COCONUT TOPPING

1 cup (60 g) unsweetened shredded coconut

Liquid food coloring of choice

## FOR THE WHIPPED CREAM

In a stand mixer fitted with the whisk, beat the heavy cream, powdered sugar, and vanilla on high speed until you reach stiff peaks, 4 to 5 minutes. Do not overmix this; otherwise, you will end up with butter!

Spoon the cooled coconut custard into a bowl and whisk until smooth and loose. Add ½ cup (120 g) of the whipped cream and whisk to loosen the mixture. Add 1 cup (240 g) of whipped cream and ¼ cup (53 g) of finely chopped tender coconut and gently fold until well combined. Pour the custard mixture into the pie crust and spread into an even layer. Top with the rest of the whipped cream and smooth into an even layer with an offset spatula.

## FOR THE SHREDDED COCONUT TOPPING

Divide the shredded coconut into three to five bowls and add 1 to 2 drops of your choice of food coloring into each bowl. Mix well until all the shredded coconut is colored. Sprinkle the colored coconut on top of the pie and refrigerate for at least 2 hours before serving.

# CINNAMON POMEGRANATE CHEESECAKE TART

This is a no-bake cheesecake tart! Well, you do have to do a little baking (the crust), but overall, it's fairly easy to make. This cheesecake has strong fall vibes and would be perfect for Thanksgiving.

I set the pomegranate arils into the cheesecake to mimic kundan jewelry. Kundan work is a traditional Indian jewelry-making technique known for its intricate craftsmanship. It is made by setting gemstones, typically uncut diamonds or precious stones, into gold foil using a technique called kundan setting. Artisans then create small, hollow settings on the jewelry piece and place each gemstone carefully within them. The gaps are then filled with molten gold to secure the stones in place. Finally, the surface is polished to reveal the stunning color of the gemstones against the rich backdrop of gold.

MAKES ONE 9-INCH (23 CM) TART

## HAZELNUT CHOCOLATE CRUST

½ cup (100 g) granulated sugar

⅔ cup (100 g) unsalted roasted hazelnuts

½ cup (60 g) all-purpose flour

⅓ cup (25 g) unsweetened cocoa powder

¼ teaspoon kosher salt

2 tablespoons unsalted butter, melted

## CHEESECAKE FILLING

7 tablespoons (105 g) heavy cream

8 ounces (225 g) cream cheese, at room temperature

½ cup (60 g) powdered sugar

¾ teaspoon ground cinnamon

¾ teaspoon vanilla extract

¼ teaspoon kosher salt

### FOR THE HAZELNUT CHOCOLATE CRUST

Preheat the oven to 325°F (160°C).

In a food processor, combine the granulated sugar, hazelnuts, flour, cocoa powder, and salt. Pulse 10 to 12 times to finely chop the hazelnuts. Pour the mixture into a bowl and add the melted butter. Mix until well combined. The mixture should have the consistency of wet sand. Pour the mixture into a 9-inch (23 cm) tart pan. Evenly press the crust into the bottom and sides of the pan.

Bake the crust for 10 minutes. Let cool completely.

### FOR THE CHEESECAKE FILLING

In a stand mixer fitted with the whisk, beat the heavy cream until you get stiff peaks, 4 to 5 minutes. Do not overmix this; otherwise, you will end up with butter! Spoon the whipped cream into a separate bowl. Swap in the paddle attachment and, to the stand mixer bowl, add the cream cheese, powdered sugar, cinnamon, vanilla, and salt. Mix for 2 minutes on high speed, scraping down the bowl halfway through. Fold in the whipped cream until well combined and there are no streaks through the cheesecake mix.

Pour the cheesecake filling into the baked tart crust and spread it into an even layer using an offset spatula. Refrigerate for 1 hour.

CONTINUED

## DARK CHOCOLATE GANACHE

3 ounces (85 g) dark chocolate, chopped (about ½ cup)

6½ tablespoons (90 ml) heavy cream

## FOR DECORATING

½ cup (175 g) pomegranate arils

Gold luster dust (optional)

### FOR THE DARK CHOCOLATE GANACHE

Place the chopped chocolate in a heatproof bowl. In a saucepan, bring the heavy cream to a simmer. Pour the hot cream over the chocolate and let it sit for 3 minutes. Whisk until you have a smooth ganache.

### TO DECORATE

Pour the ganache over the cheesecake and spread into an even layer. Arrange pomegranate arils on top of the ganache so it looks like clusters of rubies. Refrigerate the cheesecake for at least 30 minutes to 1 hour, or until the ganache sets up well.

If desired, use a fluffy brush like a blush brush to brush on gold luster dust across the top of the ganache, trying to avoid the pomegranate arils. Serve chilled.

### MAKE IT SIMPLE

Sprinkle the pomegranate arils on top of the cheesecake, rather than placing them purposefully. Dot with gold leaf and enjoy!

### NOTE

- If your ganache breaks or looks oily, add the ganache to a tall cup and use an immersion blender to blend it until it comes together.

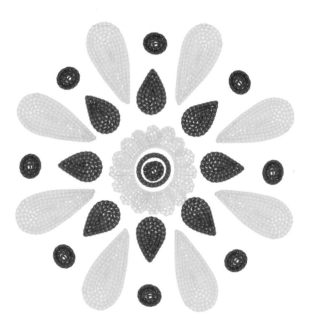

# GHUGHRA SLAB PIE

Diwali always reminds me of ghughras. Every year during Diwali, my mom and her sisters would come over to make a feast. For dessert, we would make ghughra, also known as gujiya (hand pies) filled with a mixture of khoya (milk fat), nuts, and jaggery. In this pie version of the dessert, I make a similar filling, with butter, and sandwich it between two layers of flaky buttery pastry all topped with a brown sugar glaze. I used homemade pie dough, but feel free to use store-bought pie dough if you'd like! The pie crust and the filling don't have much sugar, so the brown sugar glaze really gives it the perfect amount of sweetness. You can swap out the almonds for cashews, pecans, walnuts, or whatever nuts you have at home. Enjoy with coffee or chai!

MAKES ONE 9 × 13-INCH
(23 × 33 CM) SLAB PIE

## GHUGHRA SLAB PIE

¼ cup (35 g) unsalted roasted almonds

5 tablespoons (35 g) unsalted roasted pistachios

¼ cup (35 g) unsalted roasted hazelnuts

½ cup (100 g) granulated sugar

5 tablespoons (40 g) instant nonfat milk powder

2 tablespoons semolina (optional)

1½ tablespoons all-purpose flour

½ teaspoon ground cardamom

¼ teaspoon kosher salt

7 tablespoons (100 g) unsalted butter, at room temperature

¼ cup (60 ml) heavy cream

½ teaspoon vanilla extract

Double recipe Pie Dough (page 32), for 2 crusts

1 large egg, beaten (optional)

## BROWN SUGAR GLAZE

2 tablespoons unsalted butter

¼ cup (55 g) packed light brown sugar

1 tablespoon milk

¾ cup plus 2 tablespoons (100 g) powdered sugar

## FOR THE GHUGHRA SLAB PIE

Preheat the oven to 425°F (220°C).

In a blender, combine the almonds, pistachios, and hazelnuts and blend until you have fine crumbs. Pour the nut powder into a bowl and add the granulated sugar, milk powder, semolina (if using), flour, cardamom, and salt and whisk until well combined. Add the butter, heavy cream, and vanilla and mix until well combined. Set the filling aside.

Roll one piece of pie dough into a rectangle that is 10 × 14 inches (25 × 36 cm), or big enough to cover a shallow 9 × 13-inch (23 × 33 cm) baking pan the dough coming ½ inch (1.3 cm) up the sides of the pan. Gently lift the pie dough and place it into the baking pan. You can gently tug the dough to cover the corners if needed.

Spread the ghughra filling out into an even layer over the pie dough. Roll the second piece of dough into a 10 × 14-inch (25 × 36 cm) rectangle. Gently lift the pie dough and cover the filling. Fold the overhanging parts over and use your fingers or a fork to pinch the crusts together to seal the filling in. Use a fork to poke holes over the top of the pie to provide venting. If using, brush with the beaten egg. This helps the pie obtain a golden crust as it bakes.

Bake for 15 minutes. Reduce the oven temperature to 400°F (200°C) and bake until golden brown, another 10 minutes.

Let cool on the counter.

## FOR THE BROWN SUGAR GLAZE

Meanwhile, in a saucepan, combine the butter, brown sugar, and milk and whisk over medium heat until the brown sugar has dissolved. Pour into a bowl and whisk in the powdered sugar until you have a smooth, thick glaze.

Pour the glaze over the completely cooled pie and spread it into an even layer.

# PEAR & CARDAMOM BAKEWELL TART

Bakewell tarts are British tarts filled with a layer of strawberry jam and topped with almond frangipane. This Bakewell tart has a pear and cardamom jam base, which is super cozy and warm. I decorated the tart to mimic marble inlay, a type of art form found in Rajasthan where marble is inlaid with pieces of colored marble or precious stones. It's used to make furniture, decorative mirrors, and other home decor. Serve with tea or coffee.

**MAKES ONE 9-INCH (23 CM) TART**

Sweet Tart Dough (page 32)

3½ tablespoons (50 g) unsalted butter, at room temperature

3 tablespoons (21 g) powdered sugar, plus more for dusting

1 large egg, at room temperature

½ teaspoon almond extract

½ teaspoon vanilla extract

½ cup (51 g) almond flour

⅓ teaspoon kosher salt

3½ teaspoons all-purpose flour

½ cup (133 g) Pear & Cardamom Jam (page 28)

¼ cup (22 g) sliced almonds

Use your hands to press the tart dough into a 9-inch (23 cm) tart pan. Make sure to press the dough evenly up the sides and over the bottom of the pan. Dock the bottom and sides of the tart dough with a fork and freeze for 30 minutes or overnight.

Preheat the oven to 375°F (190°C).

Line the crust with parchment paper or foil and fill the crust with beans or pie weights. Bake the crust until the edges are lightly golden brown, 14 to 15 minutes. Remove the weights and liner and bake until lightly golden brown, an additional 8 to 9 minutes.

Let the tart shell cool.

Leave the oven on but reduce the oven temperature to 350°F (180°C).

In a stand mixer fitted with the paddle, beat the butter and powdered sugar for 2 minutes. Add the egg, almond extract, and vanilla and mix until well combined. Add the almond flour and salt and mix until well combined. Fold in the all-purpose flour, being careful not to overmix. Spoon the filling into a large piping bag and set aside.

Spread the pear and cardamom jam into an even layer on the bottom of the cooled tart shell. Cut the piping bag so that it has a 1-inch (2.5 cm) opening and pipe the filling over the jam. Use a spatula to spread the filling evenly. Place the almonds on top of the batter in an X pattern and repeat until the entire top of the tart is covered.

Bake until the top of the tart is golden brown, 30 to 33 minutes. If the edges of the tart start to get too dark, cover them with foil. Cool the tart in the pan.

To decorate, cut a piece of parchment paper into an 8-inch (20 cm) round. Place the round in the center of the tart and dust the edges of the tart with powdered sugar. Gently and carefully remove the parchment paper. Store leftovers at room temperature for 2 to 3 days or in the fridge for up to 1 week.

### SWITCH IT UP

For a pistachio Bakewell, substitute pistachio flour for the almond flour and omit the almond extract.

### MAKE IT SIMPLE

Just scatter the almonds on top rather than placing them in a pattern.

### MAKE IT EGGLESS

Make a slurry with 3 tablespoons (45 ml) whole milk and 4 teaspoons cornstarch and use in place of the egg.

# PEACH & PLUM FRANGIPANE TART

Cut fruit is the love language of most Asian parents, and my parents are no different. My parents never apologized; they'd just give me an offering of freshly cut fruit to show they cared. For this tart, I use my rough puff as a base and layer on almond frangipane with cardamom and ginger and then top it with thinly sliced plums and peaches.

MAKES ONE 9 × 13-INCH
(23 × 33 CM) TART

## PASTRY

One 9 × 13-inch (23 × 33 cm) sheet
Rough Puff (page 31)

## FRANGIPANE

½ teaspoon grated lemon zest

⅓ cup (60 g) granulated sugar

5 tablespoons (75 g) unsalted
butter, at room temperature

1 large egg, lightly beaten

½ teaspoon vanilla extract

¾ cup (72 g) almond flour

1 teaspoon ground ginger

¾ teaspoon ground cardamom

¼ teaspoon kosher salt

3 tablespoons (23 g) all-purpose
flour

## ASSEMBLY

1 large peach, cut into ¼-inch
(6 mm) slices

2 plums, cut into ¼-inch (6 mm)
slices

2 tablespoons apricot jam, warmed

1 tablespoon powdered sugar

### FOR THE PASTRY

Divide the rough puff dough in half. Store half of the dough by wrapping it in plastic wrap and freezing it.

Preheat the oven to 375°F (190°C). Line a large baking sheet with parchment paper.

Roll the remaining half of rough puff into a 9 × 13-inch (23 × 33 cm) rectangle and place on the lined baking sheet. Use a knife to lightly score a 1-inch (2.5 cm) border around the edge of the puff pastry. Use a fork to dock the center of the puff pastry (this prevents the puff pastry from puffing up too much).

Bake the puff pastry for 25 minutes so that it is parbaked.

### FOR THE FRANGIPANE

Meanwhile, in a medium bowl, combine the lemon zest and sugar. Rub the lemon zest into the sugar for 1 minute. Add the butter and mix until well combined. Add the egg and vanilla and mix for 1 minute. Add the almond flour, ground ginger, cardamom, and salt and mix until combined. Add the flour and stir until you have an even batter.

### TO ASSEMBLE

Once the pastry is done baking, remove from the oven, but leave the oven on and increase the temperature to 400°F (200°C).

Use a fork to push down the center of the puff pastry. Spread the frangipane into an even layer in the center using an offset spatula. Arrange the sliced peaches and plums on top of the frangipane.

Return to the oven and bake until the frangipane is golden brown, 35 to 40 minutes.

Immediately after the tart comes out of the oven, brush the fruit with apricot jam. Dust the tart with powdered sugar before serving.

- - - - - - - - - -

### MAKE IT EGGLESS

Substitute 3½ tablespoons (50 ml) of heavy cream or milk and 2 teaspoons of cornstarch for the egg in the frangipane.

# GAJAR KA HALWA MINI TARTS

Gajar ka halwa is every aunty's favorite dessert. It's a pudding-like dessert made with shredded carrots that are cooked down in milk and ghee with a touch of sugar and cardamom until everything is tender and melts in your mouth! You can easily find this sweet on the menus of Indian restaurants across America! These mini pies have all the flavors of gajar ka halwa in a neat little package. The filling is luscious, creamy, and reminiscent of pumpkin pie. I topped the tarts with a generous dollop of whipped cream and sprinkled on some pistachios and rose petals. Feel free to substitute jaggery for some of the granulated sugar; however, keep in mind that the color of the filling will be brown instead of orange. You can make these ahead of time and refrigerate them in an airtight container for up to 2 days before serving. Top with whipped cream right before serving.

MAKES 12 MINI TARTS

## CRUST

Double recipe Pie Dough (page 32)

## FILLING

1¼ cups (132 g) finely grated peeled carrots

⅔ cup (160 ml) evaporated milk

2 teaspoons ghee

¼ teaspoon freshly ground cardamom

4½ tablespoons (70 ml) whole milk

½ cup (100 g) granulated sugar

1 teaspoon cornstarch

1 teaspoon mawa (whole milk) powder

Pinch of salt

## FOR DECORATING

¼ cup (60 ml) heavy cream

1 tablespoon powdered sugar

½ teaspoon vanilla extract

Chopped pistachios or cashews

Dried edible flowers

## MAKE THE CRUST

Preheat the oven to 400°F (200°C).

Roll both pieces of dough to a ¼-inch (6 mm) thickness. Using a 3-inch (7.5 cm) round scalloped cookie cutter, reroll the scraps and cut out a total of 12 rounds. Gently press each round of dough into the well of a muffin tin. Press down and around the sides, making sure the dough fits snugly in each cavity. Refrigerate the pan while you make the filling.

## MAKE THE FILLING

In a saucepan, combine the grated carrots, evaporated milk, ghee, and cardamom. Stir well and bring to a boil over medium heat. Reduce the heat to low, cover, and simmer, stirring often, until the carrots are tender and soft, 10 to 15 minutes.

Transfer the cooked carrots to a blender and add the whole milk, granulated sugar, cornstarch, milk powder, and salt. Blend until smooth.

Spoon about 1½ tablespoons of the filling into each mini tart shell. Gently tap the muffin tin on the counter to smooth out the filling.

Bake until the edges of the crust are golden and the filling jiggles slightly in the center when shaken, 15 to 18 minutes.

Let the tarts cool in the pan for 10 minutes, then use a knife or offset spatula to gently lift the tarts out of the pan. Cool on a wire rack.

## TO DECORATE

In a large bowl, whisk together the heavy cream, powdered sugar, and vanilla until you have stiff peaks, 4 to 5 minutes. Do not overmix this; otherwise, you will end up with butter!

Spoon dollops of whipped cream onto the cooled pies. Sprinkle with chopped nuts and rose petals. Refrigerate until ready to serve.

# MAGAZ CREAM PIE

This is my take on a peanut butter cream pie, but it's made with magaz—aka besan ki burfi, or chickpea flour fudge. It's creamy, nutty, and ridiculously easy to make! I load my pie with a mountain of whipped cream and shards of milk chocolate, and it tastes like desi-style Reese's cups! You can make this ahead of time and refrigerate it for up to 2 days. Feel free to enjoy it straight from the fridge (or freezer for more of a cheesecake texture), or let it come to room temperature for a light, fluffy texture.

MAKES ONE 9-INCH
(23 CM) PIE

## CHOCOLATE SHORTBREAD CRUST

½ cup (60 g) all-purpose flour

⅓ cup (57 g) white rice flour

⅓ cup (28 g) almond flour

⅓ cup (28 g) unsweetened cocoa powder

⅓ cup (60 g) granulated sugar

¼ teaspoon kosher salt

6 tablespoons (85 g) unsalted butter, at room temperature

## MAGAZ CREAM FILLING

¾ cup plus 5 teaspoons (163 g) ghee

2 cups (193 g) chickpea flour

1¾ cups (198 g) powdered sugar

½ teaspoon ground cardamom

¼ teaspoon kosher salt

1⅓ cups (320 ml) heavy cream

1½ cups (322 g) mascarpone cheese, at room temperature

1 teaspoon vanilla extract

## FOR DECORATING

1 cup (240 ml) heavy cream

1 teaspoon vanilla extract

¼ cup (30 g) powdered sugar

Shaved or chopped chocolate

### FOR THE CHOCOLATE SHORTBREAD CRUST

Preheat the oven to 350°F (180°C).

In a bowl, whisk together the all-purpose flour, rice flour, almond flour, cocoa powder, granulated sugar, and salt. Add the butter and mix together with your fingers until the butter is well incorporated and the mixture holds when squeezed together with your fingertips. Spread the mixture into a 9-inch (23 cm) pie pan and press it into an even layer up the sides and over the bottom of the pan.

Bake for 15 minutes. Let the pie shell cool completely.

### FOR THE MAGAZ CREAM FILLING

Meanwhile, in a nonstick saucepan, melt the ghee over medium heat. Add the chickpea flour and mix constantly until the mixture smells nutty and has darkened in color slightly, 10 to 12 minutes.

Measure 1 cup (113 g) of the powdered sugar into a large bowl. Pour the hot chickpea mixture into the powdered sugar and add the cardamom and salt. Mix well. Be careful as the mixture is very hot! Set aside for 1 hour to cool until it's 92°F (33°C), or cool enough to touch.

While the magaz is cooling, in a large bowl, whisk the heavy cream and remaining ¾ cup (85 g) powdered sugar until you have stiff peaks. Do not overmix this; otherwise, you will end up with butter! Set aside.

In a stand mixer fitted with the whisk, beat the mascarpone cheese and vanilla until fluffy, about 2 minutes. Add the cooled magaz mixture and mix until well incorporated. Mix in one-third of the whipped cream to lighten the mixture. Fold in the rest of the whipped cream gently until there are no more white streaks.

Pour the mixture into the cooled pie crust and spread into an even layer. Refrigerate for at least 4 hours or overnight.

### TO DECORATE

In a large bowl, whisk together the cream, vanilla, and powdered sugar until you have soft peaks. Dollop the whipped cream on top and top with shaved chocolate.

# Custards & Puddings

# STRAWBERRY & JASMINE TIRAMISU

My mom has an intense green thumb, and her pride and joy is her night-blooming jasmine. Summer nights were spent sitting outside basking in the aroma of jasmine while eating freshly cut fruit from my dad. This tiramisu is an edible version of those memories, and it's made with ladyfingers that are soaked in a delicate jasmine tea and layered with ripe strawberries and a velvety mascarpone cream. Traditionally, tiramisu is made with a zabaglione, an Italian custard made with eggs, sugar, and mascarpone cheese. In this recipe, I make it eggless by using a thick mascarpone whipped cream. The tiramisu is then dusted with pink strawberry powdered sugar before serving.

MAKES ONE 8-INCH (20 CM)
SQUARE TIRAMISU

## DIPPING LIQUID

1¼ cups (300 ml) hot water

1 tablespoon honey

3 tablespoons (23 g) jasmine tea
(about 3 tea bags)

## MASCARPONE CREAM

1⅓ cups (300 g) mascarpone cheese,
cold

⅓ cup (60 g) granulated sugar

½ cup (60 g) powdered sugar

1 cup plus 6 tablespoons (320 ml)
heavy cream

1 teaspoon vanilla extract

¼ teaspoon freshly ground
cardamom

⅛ teaspoon kosher salt

## FOR ASSEMBLY

36 ladyfingers

12 ounces (340 g) strawberries,
hulled and thinly sliced (about
1 cup)

¼ cup (5 g) freeze-dried
strawberries

2½ tablespoons (18 g)
powdered sugar

### FOR THE DIPPING LIQUID

In a large bowl, stir together the hot water and honey until well combined. Add the jasmine tea and steep for 5 minutes. Strain the tea into a shallow bowl and set aside.

### FOR THE MASCARPONE CREAM

In a stand mixer fitted with the whisk, beat together the mascarpone cheese, granulated sugar, and powdered sugar for 2 minutes. Add the cream, vanilla, cardamom, and salt and whisk on medium-high speed until the mixture thickens and becomes smooth and fluffy.

### TO ASSEMBLE

Dip each ladyfinger into the tea for 2 seconds and place it into an 8-inch (20 cm) square pan. Repeat until the bottom of the pan is covered in soaked ladyfingers. Lay a single layer of sliced strawberries over the top of the ladyfingers. Spoon half the mascarpone cream mixture on top and gently spread evenly. Top with a second layer of soaked ladyfingers and strawberries. Top with the rest of the mascarpone cream. Cover with plastic wrap and refrigerate for at least 4 hours, overnight is best.

In a small blender, blend the freeze-dried strawberries and powdered sugar until fine. If you want to be a little extra fancy, you can add a pinch of edible glitter as well! Dust the top of the tiramisu with the pink powdered sugar before serving.

# SHAHI TUKDA BREAD PUDDING

Shahi tukda is a Mughal dessert made with bread toasted in ghee and then served with rabdi, sweetened milk fat spiced with cardamom and saffron. With a name like shahi tukda ("royal pieces"), you know it's a rich dessert! I took all the flavors of shahi tukda and put it into a bread pudding. I use a similar technique of shingling the bread for the bread pudding and bake it with a ricotta custard and serve it with a fat dollop of rose whipped cream. This is a great brunch dish and can be prepared the night before and baked in the morning before serving.

MAKES ONE 9-INCH (23 CM)
ROUND PAN

## BREAD PUDDING

12 to 13 thick slices brioche bread

1 ⅓ cups (320 ml) whole milk

½ cup (113 g) ricotta cheese

½ cup (100 g) granulated sugar

2 tablespoons whole milk powder

12 to 15 saffron threads

2 large eggs

¼ teaspoon ground cardamom

Pinch of salt

## FOR DECORATING

1 cup (227 g) heavy cream

¼ teaspoon rose water, store-bought or homemade (page 23)

½ cup (60 g) powdered sugar

2 tablespoons sliced almonds

2 tablespoons chopped pistachios

### FOR THE BREAD PUDDING

Preheat the oven to 350°F (180°C).

Layer the bread into a 9-inch (23 cm) round cake pan to cover the bottom.

In a bowl, whisk together the milk, ricotta, sugar, milk powder, saffron, eggs, cardamom, and salt until smooth. Pour the mixture over the brioche.

Bake until the bread pudding is set, 15 to 18 minutes.

### TO DECORATE

While the bread pudding is baking, in a bowl, whisk the heavy cream, rose water, and powdered sugar until you reach soft peaks. Do not overmix this; otherwise, you will end up with butter!

Once the bread pudding is done, sprinkle with the almonds and pistachios and serve while warm with a dollop of the rose whipped cream.

------------------------------------------------

### MAKE IT EGGLESS

Use a vegan brioche bread and a slurry of ¼ cup (60 g) of milk and 2 teaspoons of cornstarch in place of the egg in the custard.

# PHROOT SALAD

Fruit salad, which is lovingly pronounced as phroot suh-lahd by Indian families, is a mainstay at family gatherings. There are two styles of phroot salad: a thick, custardy version and a milky, soupy version. I grew up with the latter, but this recipe appeases both camps by using a milky base with rich saffron whipped cream! I know the plating of this dessert is quite extra since I used tiny cookie cutters to cut sliced fruit into little flowers. It's just an extra special touch for your guests, but if you're in a hurry, I shared an easier way to serve this dish!

MAKES 6 SERVINGS

## MILK SOUP

¾ cup (180 ml) whole milk

⅓ cup (80 ml) heavy cream

⅓ cup (80 ml) evaporated milk

6 tablespoons (117 g) sweetened condensed milk

¼ teaspoon ground cardamom

Pinch of salt

## SAFFRON WHIPPED CREAM

⅓ cup (80ml) heavy cream

2 tablespoons powdered sugar

10 saffron threads

## PHROOT SALAD

12 to 15 grapes

2 bananas, sliced

1 large apple, sliced

6 fresh figs, halved

6 tablespoons (130 g) pomegranate arils

6 tablespoons (41 g) pistachios, chopped

6 tablespoons (32 g) sliced almonds

### FOR THE MILK SOUP

In a saucepan, combine the milk, heavy cream, evaporated milk, condensed milk, cardamom, and salt. Whisk until smooth and bring to a simmer. Once it simmers, remove from the heat and refrigerate the milk mixture in an airtight container until completely cooled. You can make this 1 to 2 days in advance.

### FOR THE SAFFRON WHIPPED CREAM

In a bowl, whisk the heavy cream, powdered sugar, and saffron until you reach stiff peaks, 4 to 5 minutes. Do not overmix this; otherwise, you will end up with butter! Spoon the whipped cream into a piping bag fitted with a star tip (Ateco 864).

### FOR THE PHROOT SALAD

Use mini cookie cutters to cut the grapes, bananas, and apple into flower shapes.

Pipe dots of saffron whipped cream into six shallow bowls. Gently pour in the chilled milk soup mixture so that the tops of the whipped cream dollops are above the milk. Place your sliced fruit on top of the whipped cream and into the milk. Sprinkle on the pomegranate arils, pistachios, and almonds. Serve immediately.

--------------------------------------------

### MAKE IT SIMPLE

Cut the apple into ¼-inch (6 mm) cubes, halve the grapes, and quarter the figs. Add all the fruit to the chilled milk mixture and stir well. Ladle the fruit salad into your bowls, and use a spoon to add a dollop of whipped cream on top and sprinkle with chopped nuts.

# KADAK CHAI PANNA COTTA

At the end of a long day hanging out with my extended family, my dad always asks for a cup of Kadak chai, or strong tea. The tannins from the tea give this dessert a bittersweet flavor that I really love. Panna cotta is traditionally made with gelatin; however, to make it vegetarian, I used agar-agar to set the custard. You can find agar-agar—sometimes labeled China glass or kanten—at your local Asian grocery store or on Amazon. I highly recommend using CTC black tea for the authentic Kadak chai experience. I top my Kadak chai with Parle-G cookies, an Indian biscuit that's commonly eaten with chai in India! Every Indian mom carries a packet of Parle-G cookies in their purse for their kids, and it's a favorite childhood treat for many South Asians. If you can't get your hands on Parle-G cookies, you can use digestive biscuits or my Ginger & Jaggery Spritz Cookies (page 75) instead.

MAKES 4 SERVINGS

2 cups (480 ml) heavy cream

¼ cup (32 g) CTC loose black tea or 4 tea bags

3 tablespoons (37 g) granulated sugar, or to taste

½ teaspoon ground cardamom

½ teaspoon agar-agar powder

Whipped cream, crumbled Parle-G cookies, or melted chocolate, for serving

In a saucepan, combine the heavy cream, tea, sugar, and cardamom. Stir over medium heat for 4 minutes. Add the agar-agar and constantly whisk until the mixture comes to a boil (185°F/85°C). Reduce the heat and simmer for 3 minutes. Strain the mixture into a large cup with a spout.

Slowly pour the mixture into four 6-ounce (170 ml) containers, such as teacups, and refrigerate until set, 1 to 2 hours.

Enjoy with a dollop of whipped cream, crumbled Parle-G cookies, or a drizzle of chocolate!

# RASPBERRY ROSE LEMON POSSET

My favorite kind of Indian desserts are custards and creams. I can remember savoring silky smooth shrikhand and rich warm kheer during big holiday dinner. Possets give me the same type of feel. They are a citrus-flavored (usually lemon) dessert that has a texture similar to pudding or pot de crème but without eggs! This posset would fit right in on a Holi dessert table, when desserts like rabdi (thickened sweet cream), thandai (milk mixed with nuts and spices), and ghughra (nut-filled hand pies) are typically served.

Possets are made possible by the reaction between the cream and acid from the lemon juice. The cream is first boiled so that a good amount of water content is evaporated, and the majority of the cream left is fat. Then you add the acid, which will cause the protein in the cream to solidify, but the high fat content gets in the way of the protein and instead of curds you get a velvety, creamy texture! Resting and straining the custard before pouring it into the ramekins ensures that you won't develop a skin on your posset when you refrigerate it.

If you do decide to make this for a make-ahead party, just pour the custard into small shot glasses and refrigerate overnight. Decorate with whipped cream and garnishes the next day before serving!

MAKES 8 SERVINGS

2 teaspoons grated lemon zest

½ cup plus 1 tablespoon (118 g) granulated sugar

2 cups (480 ml) heavy cream

¼ cup (60 ml) fresh lemon juice

2 tablespoons raspberries, plus more for decorating

¼ teaspoon rose water, store-bought or homemade (page 23)

Pinch of salt

**FOR DECORATING**

Whipped cream

Dried rose petals

Fresh raspberries

Edible glitter

In a medium saucepan, combine the lemon zest and sugar. Rub the zest into the sugar until the sugar is wet and pale yellow. Add the heavy cream and bring to a boil over medium-high heat. Reduce the heat to medium and simmer for 10 minutes, stirring often.

Meanwhile, blend the lemon juice and raspberries together in a small blender until smooth. Strain the juice through a sieve to get rid of the raspberry seeds and set aside.

Remove the cream mixture from the heat and stir in the lemon/raspberry juice, rose water, and salt. Let the mixture cool for 15 minutes.

Strain the mixture into a measuring cup with a spout and pour the mixture into eight 4-ounce (115 ml) ramekins. Refrigerate the possets for 2 to 3 hours, or until set.

Decorate with whipped cream, dried rose petals, fresh raspberries, and a touch of edible glitter!

# Pastries

# THIKKI PURI & MANGO SHRIKHAND CANNOLI

Thikki puri is a spicy, deep-fried flatbread, which is usually served with shrikhand, a sweet, thickened yogurt spiced with saffron and cardamom. Personally, I like to dip my thikki puri in ras, a thick mango puree. That spicy, sweet combination just hits the spot! For this dessert, I made a crispy thikki puri cannoli shell and filled it with mango shrikhand, also known as aamarkhand. I use cannoli tubes to shape the puri into rounds, but you can also use foil that's been shaped into a 1-inch (2.5 cm) diameter cylinder. Or, to make it simpler, deep-fry the thikki puri rounds as is and serve with the mango shrikhand as a dip.

MAKES 18 CANNOLI

## MANGO SHRIKHAND

7 cups (1.6 kg) whole-milk yogurt

1 teaspoon freshly ground cardamom

12 to 15 saffron threads

¾ cup (85 g) powdered sugar

1 cup (104 g) mango puree

## THIKKI PURI CANNOLI SHELLS

¼ cup plus 1 teaspoon (40 g) semolina

1 cup (113 g) whole wheat flour

¾ teaspoon red chile powder

¾ teaspoon ground turmeric

¾ teaspoon cumin seeds

½ teaspoon ground cumin

½ teaspoon ground coriander

¼ teaspoon chaat masala (optional)

1 tablespoon vegetable oil

⅓ cup (80 ml) water

Neutral oil, for frying

¼ cup (30 g) chopped unsalted roasted pistachios, for decoration

### FOR THE MANGO SHRIKHAND

Line a sieve with three layers of cheesecloth and set over a bowl. Pour the yogurt into the sieve. Pull the corners of the cheesecloth and twist it tight. Place a plate on top and weigh it down with a can or jar. Refrigerate for at least 8 hours to drain; overnight is best.

The next day, remove the yogurt from the cheesecloth. Save the whey to use in soups, smoothies, or protein shakes! Transfer the yogurt to a bowl and whisk in the cardamom, saffron, powdered sugar, and mango puree. Place plastic wrap directly onto the surface of the yogurt and refrigerate for 2 hours.

### FOR THE THIKKI PURI CANNOLI SHELLS

In a bowl, whisk together the semolina, whole wheat flour, chile powder, turmeric, cumin seeds, ground cumin, coriander, and chaat masala (if using). Add the vegetable oil and rub it into the dry ingredients with your hand for 1 minute. This helps create a flaky puri. Add the water and knead for 2 minutes into a hard, tough dough. Cover with a damp paper towel, and set aside for 30 minutes.

Divide the dough into 18 equal portions (about 13 g each) and roll into balls. Roll each dough ball into a 4-inch (10 cm) round. It should be nice and thin. Wrap the round of dough around an oil-greased cannoli tube and use a little water to glue the overlapping parts together. Repeat with the remaining dough.

Set a wire rack in a sheet pan and place near the stove. Pour 2 to 3 inches (5 to 7.7 cm) of neutral oil into a deep saucepan and heat to 375°F (190°C). Working in batches of 2 to 3, making sure not to overcrowd your pan, add the thikki puri cannoli shells to the hot oil and fry until golden brown and crisp, 2 to 3 minutes. Drain on the wire rack and gently remove the cannoli tubes once cooled.

Spoon the shrikhand into a piping bag fitted with a large star tip (Ateco 230). Fill each cannoli shell with the shrikhand. Dip the exposed ends of shrikhand into the chopped pistachios. Serve immediately.

# ROSE CHAI MILLE-FEUILLES

Mille-feuille means "thousand sheets" and is a French pastry that consists of pastry cream and puff pastry. It's crispy and buttery, and this version is filled with a rich and creamy rose chai pastry cream. Mille-feuille typically is decorated with feathered icing, and I took inspiration from lacquered wood that's made in Kutch, Gujarat. Thin rods of wood are spun on a lathe while heated and lacquered with lac, an insect-derived resin, that's been colored. Lacquered wooden crafts can be found throughout India, but what makes Kutchi lacquered wood special is the feathered or zigzag patterns that are added to it, blending the bright colors into each other. I used some of my rolling pins as my color inspiration, but feel free to get creative with your own color palette!

MAKES 8 MILLE-FEUILLES

## PASTRY

Rough Puff (page 31), thawed on counter for 10 minutes

2 tablespoons powdered sugar

## ROSE CHAI PASTRY CREAM

1¾ cups (420 ml) whole milk

5 tablespoons (40 g) rose chai (see Note)

½ teaspoon vanilla extract

4 egg yolks

½ cup (100 g) granulated sugar

¼ teaspoon kosher salt

¼ cup (28 g) cornstarch

## FOR THE PASTRY

Preheat the oven to 400°F (200°C). Line two baking sheets with parchment paper or silicone baking mats.

Roll the rough puff dough out to 1⁄16 inch (2 mm) thick, about 19 × 15 inches (48 × 38 cm). Cut ½-inch (1.3 cm) off each edge of the rectangle so that you have nice 90 degree corners. Cut the dough into 24 rectangles that are 3 × 3½ inches (7.5 by 9 cm). Freeze the dough for 10 minutes. Place the rough puff rectangles onto the prepared baking sheets about 2 inches (5 cm) apart. Dust each pastry with the powdered sugar and place a parchment paper or silicone baking mat on top. Place another baking tray on top. This will help weigh the dough down so it puffs evenly.

Bake until golden brown, about 18 minutes. Remove from the oven and cool completely.

## FOR THE ROSE CHAI PASTRY CREAM

In a saucepan, combine the milk, rose chai, and vanilla and bring to a boil. Reduce the heat to low and simmer for 4 minutes. Remove from the heat, strain, and set aside to cool slightly.

Line a sheet pan with plastic wrap. In a bowl, whisk together the egg yolks, granulated sugar, salt, and cornstarch until it's pale and fluffy, 4 to 5 minutes. Whisk ½ cup (120 ml) of the warm milk mixture into the egg yolks to temper them, then add the rest of the milk until well combined. Pour it into a clean saucepan and whisk the mixture over medium-high heat until it thickens, about 5 minutes. Once the pastry cream starts to thicken, cook for an additional 2 minutes. Strain the mixture onto the lined sheet pan. Cover with plastic wrap, ensuring the plastic wrap touches the surface of the pastry cream to help prevent it from forming a skin. Cool on the counter for 10 minutes and then refrigerate until well chilled, about 1 hour.

Once the pastry cream has cooled, transfer it to a bowl and whisk until it's smooth and creamy. Spoon the pastry cream into a piping bag fitted with a small round tip (Ateco 8 plain). Set aside.

CONTINUED

## ICING

2 cups (226 g) powdered sugar

1 teaspoon vanilla extract

2½ tablespoons (40 ml) whole milk

Gel or liquid food coloring

## FOR THE ICING

In a bowl, whisk together the powdered sugar, vanilla, and milk. Split the icing into three cups and mix in your choice of 3 colors. I went with traditional golden yellow, deep blue, and bright pink. Mix well and spoon each icing into a piping bag fitted with a tiny round piping tip (Ateco 2 plain).

Working one at a time, pipe and fill a rectangle on a puff pastry rectangle with a single color of icing. Pipe stripes using the other two colors on top of the icing and drag a toothpick across the stripes of icing in alternating directions. Repeat with 7 more rectangles for a total of 8. These will be the tops of the pastries. Let the icing set for 5 minutes.

To assemble, lay out 8 plain rectangles of puff pastry on a rack. Pipe dollops of pastry cream across the tops of the puff pastry. Top with another rectangle of plain puff pastry and repeat. Top with the iced puff pastries. Serve immediately.

------------------------------------------------

### MAKE IT SIMPLE

Make one large mille-feuille. Roll the rough puff dough out to ¹⁄₁₆ inch (2 mm) thick and 22 × 15 inches (56 × 38 cm). Cut a ½-inch (1.3 cm) edge off the rectangle so that you have nice 90 degree corners. Cut the puff pastry into three 7 × 14 inch (18 × 36 cm) rectangles and bake per recipe. Decorate one puff pastry sheet with icing. Pipe half the pastry cream onto a plain sheet of puff pastry and layer another plain piece on top. Pipe the rest of the pastry cream onto the second layer of puff pastry and top it with the iced puff pastry sheet.

### MAKE IT EGGLESS

Boil the milk, tea, sugar, vanilla, cornstarch, and salt and simmer for 4 minutes. Strain the mixture and pour it back into a clean saucepan. Measure out 3 tablespoons (45 ml) of the strained milk and make a slurry with 3 tablespoons (21 g) of cornstarch. Add the slurry to the saucepan and cook over medium-high heat until it thickens. Cook for 2 minutes and remove from heat. Cool and continue with the recipe.

### NOTE

- If you don't have rose chai, add 3 tablespoons (3 g) of dried rose petals and ¼ teaspoon of rose water to the whole milk along with ¼ cup (32 g) of CTC black tea.

# FILTER COFFEE ÉCLAIRS

Filter coffee is probably the only way I actually enjoy coffee. It's made by taking finely ground chicory coffee and percolating hot water through it through a stainless-steel filter. The strained coffee is then mixed with boiling milk and sugar. The coffee is poured back and forth between two cups to create a rich, frothy milk on top. When I'm in India, if I have the option between filter coffee and chai, I always go for filter coffee! These éclairs are made with choux pastry, which always feels magical to me. You pipe out strips of dough, and it magically puffs up and hollows out in the oven!

For the decoration, I wanted to create designs reminiscent of sankheda furniture. Sankheda is a style of wooden handicraft from Gujarat, typically used to make furniture or baby swings (hichkos)—although, you can also find this style on dandiya, which are wooden sticks used in Dandiya Raas, a dance that's done during the festival of Navratri. The style is darkened teak wood that's painted gold and sometimes red or green. Sankheda furniture is often gifted during weddings, house warmings, or baby showers.

MAKES 14 ÉCLAIRS

## CHOUX PASTRY

3½ tablespoons (50 g) unsalted butter

2 tablespoons whole milk

2 tablespoons water

¼ teaspoon kosher salt

1½ teaspoons granulated sugar

7½ tablespoons (56 g) all-purpose flour

2 large eggs

1 tablespoon powdered sugar

Preheat the oven to 425°F (220°C). Line a large baking sheet with parchment paper.

### FOR THE CHOUX PASTRY

In a small heavy-bottomed saucepan, combine the butter, milk, water, salt, and sugar. Bring to a boil over medium heat. Once the mixture comes to a boil, add the flour and stir with a spatula until there is a thin film of dough on the bottom of the saucepan, about 2 minutes. Spoon the dough into a large bowl and stir vigorously for 1 minute to cool. Add the eggs and mix well. It might look curdled, but keep mixing, it'll eventually come together!

Spoon the dough into a piping bag with a large open star tip (Ateco 828) and pipe 3-inch (7.5 cm) lines about 3 inches (7.5 cm) apart on the prepared baking sheet. Use a damp, wet finger to gently press down on and smooth out any points or lumps. Dust each line of batter with the powdered sugar.

Using a spray bottle, mist the baking sheet with water once or twice. (If you don't have a spray bottle, dip your hand in water and flick droplets onto the baking sheet.) This helps the éclairs puff up.

Bake for 5 minutes, then reduce the oven temperature to 350°F (180°C) and bake until the choux pastry is golden brown, an additional 7 to 8 minutes. Do not open the oven door while they bake; you want the heat to dry out the center of the éclairs. Once baked, poke a hole on the side of each choux pastry using a toothpick. Turn off the oven and let the éclairs cool in the cooling oven until completely cold.

CONTINUED

## FILTER COFFEE PASTRY CREAM

1 cup (240 ml) whole milk

1½ teaspoons vanilla extract

2 teaspoons instant coffee

2 egg yolks

¼ cup (50 g) granulated sugar

2 tablespoons cornstarch

Pinch of salt

## FOR DECORATING

¼ cup (60 ml) heavy cream

1¾ teaspoons unsweetened cocoa powder

¼ cup (48 g) chopped semisweet chocolate

Gold luster dust

Clear alcohol (vodka, tequila, etc.)

## FOR THE FILTER COFFEE PASTRY CREAM

In a saucepan, combine the milk, vanilla, and instant coffee and bring to a boil. Remove from the heat and set aside to cool slightly.

Line a sheet pan with plastic wrap. In a medium bowl, whisk together the egg yolks, granulated sugar, cornstarch, and salt until pale and fluffy. Add ½ cup (120 ml) of the hot milk mixture to the egg yolks to temper them and whisk well. Add the remaining milk mixture and mix until well combined. Pour the mixture into a clean medium saucepan and cook over medium-high heat, whisking constantly, until the mixture starts to thicken. Once it thickens, cook for an additional 2 minutes. Strain the mixture onto the lined sheet pan. Cover with plastic wrap, ensuring the plastic wrap touches the surface of the pastry cream so that it doesn't form a skin. Cool on the counter for 10 minutes and then refrigerate until cooled completely.

Once the pastry cream has cooled, transfer to a bowl and whisk until it's smooth and creamy. Spoon the pastry cream into a piping bag fitted with a long filling tip (Ateco 230).

Make a hole using a knife that is large enough for the piping tip to fit into the éclair and fill each éclair with the filter coffee pastry cream until completely full.

### TO DECORATE

Set a wire rack in a sheet pan and set the éclairs on the rack. In a small saucepan, combine the heavy cream, cocoa powder, and semisweet chocolate and whisk over low heat until the chocolate has melted. Dip the top of each éclair into the chocolate glaze and shake off the excess. Return to the wire rack and let sit at room temperature until the chocolate sets, about 1 hour.

In a small pinch pot, mix the gold luster dust with a teaspoon of a clear alcohol. Use a fine paint brush to brush on thin and thick lines, mimicking sankheda designs. The alcohol will evaporate off, leaving the gold luster dust behind. Enjoy immediately.

- - - - - - - - - - - - - - - - - - - - - - - - - - - - - - - - - - - - - - - - - -

### NOTES

- You can make the éclair shells ahead of time and freeze them. Just toast them in the oven at 350°F (180°C) for 5 minutes and cool before filling.

- This recipe cannot be made eggless as the eggs allow the choux pastry to hollow out as it bakes.

# KESAR PISTA CREAM PUFFS

These colorful cream puffs are an ode to the quintessential desi flavor combo, kesar and pista (saffron and pistachios). These cream puffs are filled with Chantilly cream, a fancy word for homemade whipped cream, flavored with saffron, cardamom, and small pieces of pistachios. The cream puffs are all topped with a bright marbled craquelin. Craquelin is a mixture of flour and sugar that is rolled out thinly and placed on top of the pastry before baking. After baking, it turns into this crisp crackled top. I love how bright and festive these cream puffs are with the craquelin, but if you want to shorten the recipe, you can totally skip it. On another note, be sure to fill the cream puffs right before serving, or the pastry will get soggy. Also, you can freeze the empty cream puffs for up to 6 months.

MAKES 24 CREAM PUFFS

## COLORED CRAQUELIN

4 tablespoons (60 g) unsalted butter, at room temperature

2 tablespoons plus 1½ teaspoon (33 g) light brown sugar

2½ tablespoons (31 g) granulated sugar

½ cup (60 g) all-purpose flour

Gel food coloring (Wilton rose, neon blue, and neon green)

## CHOUX PASTRY

3½ tablespoons (50 ml) unsalted butter

3½ tablespoons (50 ml) whole milk

3½ tablespoons (50 g) water

1 teaspoon granulated sugar

¼ teaspoon kosher salt

½ teaspoon vanilla extract

9 tablespoons (67 g) all-purpose flour

2 large eggs

Preheat the oven to 375°F (190°C). Line a large baking sheet with parchment paper.

### FOR THE COLORED CRAQUELIN

In a bowl, mix together the butter, brown sugar, granulated sugar, and flour until you have a well-combined dough. Split the dough into 3 equal portions. Knead your choice of food coloring into each dough until you have an even color.

Roll each dough color into a log and place the logs next to each other lengthwise. Then cut in half horizontally and place one half diagonally on top of the bottom half. Press together and roll until it is ⅛ inch (3 mm) thick. Place in the freezer.

### FOR THE CHOUX PASTRY

In a small heavy-bottom saucepan, combine the butter, milk, water, sugar, salt, and vanilla. Bring to a boil over medium heat. Once the mixture comes to a boil, add the flour and stir with a spatula until there is a thin film of dough on the bottom and sides of the saucepan, about 1 minute. Spoon dough into a large bowl and stir vigorously for 3 to 4 minutes to help cool down the mixture. Add the eggs and mix well after each addition until you have a smooth dough.

Spoon the dough into a piping bag and fit it with a large round tip (Wilton 809). Hold the piping bag directly above the lined baking sheet (at a 90-degree angle) and pipe out 1½-inch (4 cm) dollops about 2 inches (5 cm) apart. Use a 1½-inch (4 cm) round cookie cutter to cut rounds out of the cold craquelin dough and place a round on top of each dollop of choux pastry. Using a spray bottle, mist the baking sheet with water once or twice. (Alternatively, dip your hand in a little water and flick droplets onto the baking sheet.)

CONTINUED

## KESAR PISTA CHANTILLY CREAM

2 cups (480 ml) heavy cream

½ teaspoon saffron

¾ teaspoon freshly ground cardamom

⅓ cup (38 g) powdered sugar

½ cup (50 g) finely chopped pistachios

Bake for 15 minutes and then increase the temperature to 400°F (200°C). Bake the choux pastry until the bottom of the pastry has browned but the craquelin has not, 5 to 8 minutes. Use a toothpick to poke a hole into the side of each cream puff. Turn the oven off and return the baking sheet to the oven, leaving the door slightly open, and keep it in the oven for 1 hour to help dry out the inside of the choux pastry.

### FOR THE KESAR PISTA CHANTILLY CREAM

In a large bowl, combine the heavy cream, saffron, and cardamom. Stir and refrigerate for 15 minutes to allow the flavors to bloom. Add the powdered sugar and whip until you have stiff peaks, 4 to 5 minutes. Fold in the chopped pistachios.

Spoon the Chantilly cream into a piping bag and snip off a ½-inch (1.3 cm) tip. Fill the cream puffs by poking a hole into the bottom of each cream puff with a small knife and filling it with the cream until it's full. Wipe off any excess whipped cream and place on a tray to serve.

- - - - - - - - - - - - - - - - - - - - - - - - - - - - - - - - - - - - - - -

### NOTE

•  This recipe cannot be made eggless as the eggs allow the choux pastry to hollow out as it bakes.

# TIL CHIKKI BOMBAY-BREST

These Bombay-Brests are a desi version of Paris-Brest, a French choux-based pastry that's filled with praline crème mousseline. Praline is made from nuts that are coated in caramelized sugar and then blended into a paste. The praline in a Paris-Brest is typically made with almonds, hazelnuts, or other nuts, but for my Bombay-Brest, I use til chikki, or sesame seed brittle. Chikki is any brittle made with jaggery powder and sugar. You can also use peanuts instead to make a peanut chikki Bombay-Brest!

MAKES 10 PASTRIES

## CHOUX PASTRY

7 tablespoons (100 g) unsalted butter

6½ tablespoons (100 ml) whole milk

6½ tablespoons (100 ml) water

1 tablespoon granulated sugar

¼ teaspoon kosher salt

1 teaspoon vanilla extract

1 cup (120 g) all-purpose flour

4 large eggs

1 tablespoon powdered sugar

## TIL CHIKKI PRALINE

3 tablespoons (30 g) sesame seeds

1 tablespoon water

2½ tablespoons (30 g) jaggery

2½ tablespoons (31 g) granulated sugar

½ teaspoon kosher salt

1 tablespoon coconut oil

2 tablespoons cookie butter or almond butter

Preheat the oven to 425°F (220°C). Line a baking sheet with parchment paper. Make a piping guide by tracing 10 circles with a pencil, using a 3-inch (7.5 cm) round cookie cutter as a template, onto the parchment paper 2 inches (5 cm) apart. Flip the parchment paper over so the pencil side is down on the baking pan. Set aside.

### FOR THE CHOUX PASTRY

In a small heavy-bottomed saucepan, combine the butter, milk, water, granulated sugar, salt, and vanilla. Bring to a boil over medium heat. Once the mixture comes to a boil, add the flour and stir with a spatula until there is a thin film of dough on the bottom and sides of the saucepan, about 1 minute. Spoon the dough into a large bowl and stir vigorously for 3 to 4 minutes to help cool down the mixture. Add the eggs and mix well after each addition until you have a smooth dough, 3 to 4 minutes.

Spoon the dough into a piping bag and fit it with a large star tip (Ateco 230). Holding the piping bag directly above the parchment-lined baking sheet, pipe dough over the guides that you traced earlier. Dust the top of each dough with the powdered sugar. Using a spray bottle, mist the baking sheet with water once or twice. (Alternatively, dip your hand in a little water and flick droplets onto the baking sheet.)

Bake the choux pastry until the pastry has puffed up and browned, 20 to 23 minutes. Turn the oven off and keep the baking sheet in the oven for 1 hour to help dry out the inside of the choux pastry.

### FOR THE TIL CHIKKI PRALINE

In a dry skillet, toast the sesame seeds over medium-high heat while constantly stirring until fragrant and nutty, 8 to 10 minutes. Pour the sesame seeds into a bowl and cool completely.

CONTINUED

## CRÈME MOUSSELINE

1 cup (240 ml) whole milk

1½ teaspoons vanilla extract

2 large egg yolks

⅓ cup (60 g) granulated sugar

2 tablespoons cornstarch

9½ tablespoons (133 g) unsalted butter, at room temperature

2 tablespoons powdered sugar, for dusting

Line a baking sheet with parchment paper or a silicone baking mat.

In a small 1 quart (950 ml) saucepan, combine the water, jaggery, granulated sugar, and salt and bring to a boil. Do not mix or whisk the caramel; gently swirl the pan every few minutes to help evenly cook the caramel. Brush the sides of the pan down with a wet paper towel as needed to help prevent crystallization. Simmer for 8 minutes, or until it reaches 300°F (150°C). Remove from the heat, add the sesame seeds, and mix well. Pour the sesame seed brittle onto the prepared baking sheet and spread into a thin layer. Let the brittle cool completely before breaking into small pieces.

In a food processor or blender, process the cooled brittle for 1 minute on high speed. Add the coconut oil and cookie butter and blend until it is as smooth as possible.

### FOR THE CRÈME MOUSSELINE

In a saucepan, combine the milk and vanilla and bring to simmer. Remove from the heat. In a small bowl, whisk together the egg yolks, granulated sugar, and cornstarch until pale and fluffy. Add ½ cup (120 ml) of the warm milk to the egg mixture and whisk until well combined. Pour the egg mixture back into the saucepan with the milk and cook over high heat, whisking constantly until the mixture thickens. Once the cream thickens, cook for an additional 2 minutes. Strain the mixture onto a plate and cover with plastic wrap. Freeze the pastry cream for 30 minutes, or until completely cool.

In a stand mixer fitted with the paddle, beat the butter and 3 tablespoons (66 g) of praline on high speed for 4 minutes. Scrape down the bowl and add the pastry cream 1 tablespoon at a time while mixing on low speed. Once all the pastry cream has been incorporated, mix on high speed for 3 minutes. Spoon the crème mousseline into a piping bag fitted with a large star tip (Ateco 230).

To assemble the desserts, cut the choux pastry horizontally in half. Pipe a small amount of the remaining til chikki praline into the bottom of each pastry, pipe a ring of mousseline on top, and then pipe dollops of mousseline on top of the ring so that you have two layers of mousseline. Place the top half of the pastry on top and dust with powdered sugar before serving.

# GULAB JAMUN BABAS

This is a mash-up of baba au rhum and gulab jamun, two sweet doughs that are soaked in sugar syrups. Baba au rhum is an enriched bread soaked in a rum and orange syrup and topped with whipped cream. It's light, boozy, and similar to gulab jamun, extremely rich. Gulab jamun is probably the most common dessert you'll see on menus at Indian restaurants. It's deep-fried milk-fat donuts that are soaked in a cinnamon, cardamom, and rose syrup. They're aromatic and sticky sweet! In this recipe, I don't use any alcohol, but feel free to make it a proper baba au rhum by adding a drizzle of rum on top after soaking it in the syrup.

MAKES 12 GULAB JAMUN BABAS

## DOUGH

1¼ cup (150 g) all-purpose flour

½ teaspoon instant yeast

½ teaspoon kosher salt

1 teaspoon honey

4 tablespoons (60 g) unsalted butter, at room temperature

4 large eggs

Softened butter, for the molds

## SYRUP

1 cup (240 ml) water

½ cup (100 g) granulated sugar

10 cardamom pods, lightly crushed

10 to 12 saffron threads

2 teaspoons rose water, store-bought or homemade (page 23)

## FOR DECORATING

1½ cups (360 ml) heavy cream

½ cup (60 g) powdered sugar

2 teaspoons vanilla extract

Chopped pistachios (optional)

Rose petals (optional)

## FOR THE DOUGH

In a stand mixer fitted with the dough hook, combine the flour, yeast, salt, honey, and butter and mix on medium speed until it has a coarse sandy texture, about 3 minutes. Add the eggs and mix for 10 minutes on high speed, scraping down the bowl often. The dough will be very loose and soft.

Grease the cups of a muffin tin or twelve 4-ounce (115ml) jars with butter and place them on a baking sheet. Add about ¼ cup (28 g) of dough to each cup. The dough will be quite sticky, so use damp hands to portion the dough. Cover loosely with plastic wrap and proof until the dough doubles in size, 1 to 1½ hours.

Preheat the oven to 375°F (190°C).

Bake the babas until golden brown, about 15 minutes.

Let cool for 5 minutes in the pan, then transfer to a wire rack to cool.

## FOR THE SYRUP

Meanwhile, in a saucepan, combine the water, sugar, and cardamom pods and bring to a boil over medium-high heat. Simmer for 4 minutes and strain the syrup into a bowl. Add the saffron and rose water and cool the syrup for 10 minutes.

Add 2 to 3 babas at a time to the saucepan of syrup. Let it soak for 3 to 4 minutes.

## TO DECORATE

In a bowl, whisk together the cream, powdered sugar, and vanilla until you have soft peaks. Do not overmix this; otherwise, you will end up with butter! Pipe whipped cream on each baba and, if desired, top with a sprinkle of pistachios and rose petals!

# PURAN POLI SWIRL BREAD

Every Diwali my mom makes puran poli, a sweet flatbread stuffed with a sweetened chickpea filling. I loved the idea of having a swirl of the filling in a loaf of milk bread for a Diwali morning breakfast with chai! The puran poli filling in this recipe isn't traditional because I use butter instead of ghee and it's a bit looser than a traditional filling, which made it easier to spread over the dough. The bread is mildly sweet and gives you all the puran poli vibes with half the work! I like to enjoy slices of my puran poli swirl bread with butter, ghee, or some chai!

MAKES ONE 8 × 4-INCH
(20 × 10 CM) LOAF

## PURAN POLI FILLING

½ cup (111 g) chana dal (split chickpeas), rinsed

¼ teaspoon ground turmeric

⅔ cup (110 g) jaggery

2 tablespoons unsalted butter, at room temperature

2 tablespoons (27 g) light brown sugar

¼ teaspoon ground cardamom

Pinch of salt

## BREAD

2¼ teaspoons (7 g) active dry yeast (1 envelope)

½ cup (120 ml) warm water, at least 110°F (43°C)

½ cup (120 ml) warm milk, at least 110°F (43°C)

2 tablespoons vegetable oil, plus more for brushing

1 tablespoon granulated sugar

1½ teaspoons kosher salt

2¾ cups plus 1½ tablespoons (341 g) all-purpose flour

Softened butter, for the loaf pan

1 tablespoon (15 g) unsalted butter, melted

### FOR THE PURAN POLI FILLING

In a saucepan, combine the rinsed dal, turmeric, and 2 cups (480 ml) water and bring to a boil. Reduce to a simmer and cook until the dal is soft, tender, and easily mashed between your fingers, about 30 minutes.

Drain the dal and add it to a skillet along with the jaggery. Cook over medium heat. As the jaggery melts, mash the dal with a spatula. Once all the jaggery has melted, transfer the mixture to a blender and blend until smooth. Pour the mixture into a bowl and mix in the butter, brown sugar, cardamom, and salt until well combined. Let the mixture cool.

### FOR THE BREAD

In a large bowl, whisk together the yeast, warm water, warm milk, oil, granulated sugar, and salt. Rest for 5 minutes. Add the flour and use a spatula to bring the dough together. Once it's shaggy, use your hands to knead the dough for 5 minutes. The dough will be slightly tacky. If it feels too sticky, wash your hands and go back to the dough. If it's still sticky, dust with flour as needed. Place the dough ball into a greased bowl and proof the dough in a warm place until it doubles in size, about 1 hour.

Once the dough has doubled in size, roll it out to a 7 × 14-inch (18 × 36 cm) rectangle. If the dough keeps shrinking, let it rest for 5 minutes and try again.

Butter an 8 × 4-inch (20 × 10 cm) loaf pan. Spread the puran poli filling out over the dough in a thin even layer. With a short side facing you, roll the dough up, pinching the sides as you roll to seal. Place the log seam-side down in the greased pan. Brush the top with a little oil and cover with plastic wrap. Proof for 30 minutes.

Preheat the oven to 400°F (200°C.) Bake the bread until the center of the loaf registers 190°F (88°C), 30 to 40 minutes.

Once done, brush the top with the melted butter. Let cool for 5 minutes in the pan and then flip onto a wire rack to cool completely.

# CHUM CHUM MARITOZZI

As a kid, chum chums, a Bengali mithai (sweet), were hard to resist when I was at the mithai shops. Chum chums are brightly colored balls of chhena, or paneer, soaked in sugar syrup and then split in half and filled with mawa, or boiled down milk solids. When I saw maritozzi, Italian sweet rolls filled with whipped cream, becoming a trendy dessert, they reminded me of chum chums! I baked fluffy pink rolls and filled them with saffron ricotta whipped cream. This bread is made with a Japanese technique that uses tangzhong, or a roux made with bread flour and milk. It helps hydrate the flour, which leads to more steam, creating a fluffy bread. It's light, not too sweet (aka parent-approved), and perfect for a picnic!

MAKES 12 MARITOZZI

## TANGZHONG

⅓ cup (80 ml) whole milk

¼ cup (30 g) bread flour

## MARITOZZI BREAD

7 tablespoons (80 ml) whole milk, warm

2½ tablespoons (30 g) granulated sugar

2½ tablespoons (56 g) honey

1 large egg

1 large egg yolk

1½ teaspoons (5 g) instant or active dry yeast

¾ teaspoon vanilla extract

Pink food coloring (optional)

2¾ cups (330 g) bread flour

2½ tablespoons (20 g) milk powder

½ teaspoon freshly ground cardamom

¼ teaspoon kosher salt

2½ tablespoons (34 g) olive oil, plus more for the bowl

1 egg yolk, beaten

2 tablespoons unsweetened shredded coconut

### FOR THE TANGZHONG

In a saucepan, combine the bread flour and milk and whisk over medium-low heat until it starts to thicken, about 30 seconds. It should be thick enough so that your whisk leaves a trail when stirring. Remove from the heat and let cool.

### FOR THE MARITOZZI BREAD

In a stand mixer fitted with the whisk, beat together the milk, granulated sugar, honey, whole egg, egg yolk, yeast, vanilla, and pink food coloring (if using). Whisk well and let it rest for 5 minutes. Add the bread flour, milk powder, cardamom, and salt and mix by hand with a spatula until you have a shaggy dough. Snap on the dough hook and mix on medium-high speed for 8 minutes, scraping down the bowl halfway through. The dough will be very sticky. Slowly drizzle in the olive oil and mix until it's completely incorporated, about 3 minutes.

Grease a large bowl with olive oil and place the dough into the bowl. Cover the dough with a tea towel and place in a warm place to rise until it has doubled in size, 1 to 1½ hours.

Line a baking sheet with parchment paper or a silicone baking mat. Punch down the dough and divide the dough into 12 equal portions (60 g each). Roll each piece of dough into a ball by cupping your hands around each dough ball and rolling it against a clean surface in a circular motion. Place the dough balls on the prepared baking sheet 3 inches (7.5 cm) apart. Cover with plastic wrap and proof until they double in size, about 1 hour.

Preheat the oven to 375°F (190°C).

Brush the top of each bun with some the beaten egg yolk and sprinkle on the shredded coconut.

Bake until golden brown or the center of the rolls reach 185°F (85°C), 9 to 10 minutes.

Transfer the rolls to a wire rack to cool.

CONTINUED

## SUGAR SYRUP

⅓ cup (80 ml) water

¼ cup (50 g) granulated sugar

## SAFFRON RICOTTA WHIPPED CREAM

1 cup (240 ml) heavy cream

⅓ cup (85 g) full-fat ricotta cheese

½ cup (60 g) powdered sugar

½ teaspoon vanilla extract

10 to 12 saffron threads

## ASSEMBLY

⅓ cup (36 g) unsalted roasted pistachios, coarsely chopped

### FOR THE SUGAR SYRUP

Meanwhile, in a saucepan, bring the water and sugar to a boil. Simmer for 2 minutes and remove from the heat. Set aside to cool.

### FOR THE SAFFRON RICOTTA WHIPPED CREAM

In a bowl, combine the cream, ricotta, powdered sugar, vanilla, and saffron and whisk until stiff peaks have formed, 4 to 5 minutes. Do not overmix this; otherwise, you will end up with butter! Spoon the mixture into a piping bag and cut a ½-inch (1.3 cm) tip.

### TO ASSEMBLE

Use a serrated knife to cut each roll down the center without cutting all the way through. Gently open the cut and brush the inside with the sugar syrup. Use the piping bag to fill the cut with the saffron ricotta whipped cream. Use an offset spatula to smooth out the whipped cream and remove any excess. Sprinkle each maritozzi with chopped pistachios. Serve immediately.

--------------------------------------------------

### MAKE IT EGGLESS

Use 4¼ tablespoons (64 g) of unsalted butter, room temperature, in place of the egg and egg yolk in the dough and use an additional ½ teaspoon of yeast. You can use 1 tablespoon of milk or heavy cream instead of an egg wash.

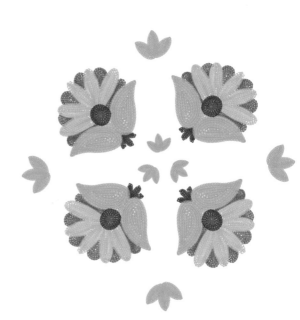

# PAINTED BLUE POTTERY BREAD

When painted loaves of bread by Allison Loveall popped up in my social media feed, I knew I had to make one! This turmeric-swirled sourdough is painted with a mix of blue food coloring and liquid white food coloring to look like Jaipur blue pottery. The blue pottery from Jaipur is special in that it's painted with distinct bright sky and cobalt blues. I hand-painted floral and geometric patterns on the bread before baking, similar to how artisans paint them before putting them in the kiln.

To get the vibrant colors to show up on the bread, I mix the gel food coloring with white food coloring. This makes the colors more opaque and allows them to really pop once baked!

**MAKES ONE 8-INCH (20 CM) LOAF**

2½ cups (300 g) bread flour

1½ teaspoons sugar

1 teaspoon instant yeast

1 teaspoon kosher salt

¾ cup plus 2 teaspoons (190 ml) warm water (90° to 110°F/32° to 43°C)

½ teaspoon ground turmeric

Liquid white food coloring

Blue food coloring

In the bowl of a stand mixer, combine the flour, sugar, yeast, salt, and water. Use a spatula to mix the ingredients until you have a shaggy dough. Snap on the dough hook and knead the dough for 6 minutes. Split the dough in half and add the turmeric to one of the halves. Knead the turmeric in until the dough is light yellow without any pockets of dry turmeric. Place the turmeric-colored dough ball into a greased bowl. Knead the second dough ball for 2 minutes and place the dough ball on top of the turmeric dough. Cover the bowl with plastic wrap and let the dough rise or until doubled in size, about 2 hours.

Line a baking sheet with parchment paper. Turn the dough out onto a lightly floured surface so that the turmeric dough is on the top and deflate the dough. Roll the dough into a log and press it into a little rectangle. Gather the edges and pinch them together. Flip the dough ball over and gently roll the dough along the work surface to seal and tighten the dough ball. Place the dough ball on the prepared pan, cover with plastic wrap, and proof the dough until doubled in size, 45 minutes to 1 hour.

About 15 minutes before the dough is done proofing, preheat the oven to 450°F (230°C). Add a cast-iron pan with 1½ cups (360 ml) of boiling water to the bottom rack of the oven.

Add 4 to 5 drops of liquid white food coloring to each of three small bowls. Leave one bowl white. Add blue food coloring to a second bowl to make sky blue. Make the third bowl dark blue.

Lightly dust the proofed dough with flour. Using a thin paint brush, paint the bread with white food coloring to create a floral design. I suggest magnifying the motifs so that they are larger so you don't lose the details once it bakes. Paint the background sky blue and use the dark blue to outline the white floral motifs. Use a sharp knife to cut a slash ½ inch (1.3 cm) deep across the bread.

Bake until the center of the bread registers 195°F (91°C), 23 to 25 minutes. Cool the bread on a rack for 1 hour before cutting.

# Frozen
# Desserts

# MULBERRIES & CARDAMOM CREAM ICE CREAM

Mulberries, or śētūra, hold a very special place in my heart. My maternal grandparents lived with me when I was little, and although we had some trouble communicating due to our language differences, we always could agree on food. My grandfather discovered a mulberry tree in our local ShopRite parking lot, and we'd trek over a mile to the parking lot to enjoy them. My grandfather would put me on his shoulders so I could reach the ripe berries and stuff my mouth. It became a tradition of sorts during the early summer months. Sadly, a few years later, they cut down the tree to put up a bigger parking lot, but I still remember walking home with my grandfather with my face covered in sweet, purple mulberry juice with my sticky hands tucked tightly into his. For this ice cream, you can use frozen or fresh mulberries. However, if you can't find them, any berry will work in this recipe!

MAKES 1 QUART (960 ML) ICE CREAM

### MULBERRY JAM

4 ounces (115 g) frozen mulberries

1½ tablespoons fresh lemon juice

⅓ cup (60 g) granulated sugar

### SWEET CARDAMOM CREAM

2 cups (480 ml) heavy cream

1 cup (312 g) sweetened condensed milk

1 teaspoon vanilla extract

¾ teaspoon ground cardamom

¼ teaspoon kosher salt

### ICE CREAM

5 to 6 graham crackers or 12 Parle-G biscuits, coarsely crushed

### FOR THE MULBERRY JAM

In a saucepan, combine the mulberries, lemon juice, and sugar. Cook over medium heat until the mixture registers 220°F (104°C), 14 to 18 minutes. Strain the mixture through a sieve into a bowl to get rid of any seeds. Set aside to cool completely.

### FOR THE SWEET CARDAMOM CREAM

In a stand mixer fitted with the whisk, beat the heavy cream on high speed until it forms soft peaks, 4 to 5 minutes. Add the sweetened condensed milk, vanilla, cardamom, and salt and mix for an additional 3 minutes, or until well combined.

### FOR THE ICE CREAM

Pour half the cream mixture into an 8 × 4 inch (20 × 10 cm) loaf pan and add half the mulberry jam and half the crushed cookies and swirl it in with a knife. Add the remaining cream mixture and top with the rest of the jam and cookies and swirl the jam in. Cover and freeze over-night before serving.

# COCONUT DATE & WALNUT MILKSHAKE

This is another mash-up of my grown-up and childhood favorites! In the summers my masi (mom's sister) would make chickoo (sapote or sapodilla) milkshakes for any guests that would come over, and I LOVED them. I'd always ask for her to make an extra portion just for me! As a grown-up, I also became obsessed with Hadley Fruit Orchards date shakes in Palm Springs. I love how rich and creamy they are, and they have that lightly sweet, caramelly flavor from the dates, similar to the flavor of chickoo.

MAKES 4 TO 6 SERVINGS

1 young coconut
½ cup (120 ml) whole milk
½ teaspoon vanilla extract
¼ teaspoon kosher salt
3 Medjool dates, pitted
1½ cups (321 g) vanilla ice cream
2½ tablespoons (20 g) walnuts
Whipped cream (optional)

To open the coconut, use a sharp chef's knife to shave off the top of the coconut until you see the lines on the hard shell of the coconut. Use the heel of the knife to hit a circle around the top of the exposed coconut. Peel the top part off and drain the coconut water into a cup. Use a spoon to scoop out the tender coconut meat.

In a blender, combine ½ cup (120 ml) coconut water, 1 cup (212 g) coconut meat, the milk, vanilla, salt, dates, ice cream, and walnuts. Blend until smooth and serve immediately. Feel free to top it with some whipped cream!

# CASSATA ICE CREAM CAKE

One of my mom's favorite frozen desserts is cassata! Cassata is a layered ice cream cake that is traditionally from Sicily, but it's wildly popular in India as well. In India, the ice cream cake is layers of tutti frutti (candied fruit), pistachio, and mango ice cream. Sometimes it has a cake layer, sometimes it doesn't, and they're delicious no matter what! In my cassata, I use fresh cherries for the pink layer since tutti frutti can be hard to find.

MAKES ONE 8 × 4-INCH (20 × 10 CM)
ICE CREAM CAKE

1½ cups (360 ml) heavy cream

¾ cup (234 g) sweetened condensed milk

1 teaspoon vanilla extract

3 tablespoons (47 g) cherry puree

3 tablespoons (36 g) coarsely chopped cherries

½ cup (54 g) pistachios, coarsely chopped

Green food coloring (optional)

¼ cup (26 g) mango puree

## FOR DECORATING

½ cup (120 ml) heavy cream

2 tablespoons powdered sugar

½ teaspoon vanilla extract

Chopped nuts, sprinkles, chocolate shavings, edible flowers, etc. (optional)

Line an 8 × 4-inch (20 × 10 cm) loaf pan with parchment paper so that you have large overhang on each side.

In a stand mixer fitted with the whisk, beat the heavy cream on medium-high speed until you reach soft peaks, about 3 minutes. Add the sweetened condensed milk and vanilla and mix for 3 minutes on high speed until smooth and thick. Divide the ice cream mixture evenly among three bowls (about 194 g per bowl). Add the cherry puree and chopped cherries to one bowl. Add half of the chopped pistachios and some green food coloring (if using) to a second bowl. Add the mango puree to the last bowl. Mix each flavor until well blended.

Pour the cherry ice cream mixture into the loaf pan and spread it into an even layer. Gently spoon the pistachio mixture on top and spread into a smooth layer. Top with the mango layer. Sprinkle the top with the remaining pistachios and freeze overnight.

## TO DECORATE

In a bowl, whisk the cream, powdered sugar, and vanilla until it reaches stiff peaks, 4 to 5 minutes. Do not overmix this; otherwise, you will end up with butter! Use the parchment paper overhang to lift the cake out of the pan and onto a plate. Pipe dollops of whipped cream on top. If desired, decorate with nuts, sprinkles, chocolate shavings, or edible flowers before serving.

# GOLAS (SNOW ICE)

Summertime is gola time! Gola carts (shaved ice carts) with bottles of colorful syrups can be found all over the streets of India during the summer. You won't find your typical snow ice flavors like strawberry or lemon, but you'll find spiced syrups like kala khatta, a syrup based on jamun (java plum) and spiced with cumin. Since jamun can be tough to find, I used ripe, juicy Bing cherries instead, which provide a ton of sweetness. For the lime and fennel syrup, you can omit the fennel in the lime syrup if you want a simpler flavor.

To make your golas, you can either use a snow ice maker, if you have one, or a blender. Add 4 cups (870 g) of ice to a high-powered blender and blend until you have small shards of ice. Spoon the snow ice into a bowl and top with your choice of syrups!

EACH SYRUP MAKES 2 CUPS
(480 ML)

## CHERRY KALA KHATTA SYRUP

2½ cups (500 g) cherry puree

1 cup (200 g) granulated sugar

1½ teaspoons black salt (kala namak)

1½ teaspoons ground cumin

6 tablespoons (90 ml) fresh lemon juice

## LIME AND FENNEL SYRUP

1 cup (240 ml) fresh lime juice

1½ cups (300 g) granulated sugar

½ teaspoon fennel seeds, coarsely ground

## MANGO SYRUP

1 cup (240 ml) mango juice

1 cup (200 g) granulated sugar

3 tablespoons (45 ml) fresh lime juice

### FOR THE CHERRY KALA KHATTA SYRUP

In a saucepan, combine the cherry puree, sugar, black salt, and cumin and bring to a boil. Simmer for 2 minutes and strain the mixture into a container. Stir in the lemon juice and let cool completely before using.

### FOR THE LIME AND FENNEL SYRUP

In a saucepan, combine ¾ cup (180 ml) of the lime juice, the sugar, and fennel seeds and bring to a boil. Simmer for 1 minute. Remove from the heat and stir in the remaining ¼ cup (60 ml) of lime juice. Strain and cool completely before using.

### FOR THE MANGO SYRUP

In a saucepan, combine the mango juice and sugar and bring to a boil. Simmer for 1 minute. Remove from the heat and stir in the lime juice. Cool completely before using.

Store the syrups in airtight containers in the fridge for up to 1 month or in the freezer for 6 months.

# MANGO LIME MINT SORBET

Growing up in New Jersey, summers meant loads and loads of fresh Italian ice! Sadly, it's hard to find in the Bay Area, so I like to make the next best thing: sorbet! This mango sorbet is refreshing, light, and extremely easy to make. I love serving a scoop of this sorbet in a glass of sparkling wine, like prosecco or champagne, for fancy brunches!

MAKES 1 PINT (480 ML)

1 cup (200 g) granulated sugar

15 fresh mint leaves

2 teaspoons grated lime zest

2⅔ cups (300 ml) water

1¼ cups (270 g) mango puree

¼ cup (60 ml) fresh lime juice

In a saucepan, combine the sugar, mint leaves, and lime zest and use your hands to rub the mixture together for 1 minute. Add the water, bring to a boil, then reduce to a simmer and cook until the sugar has dissolved. Remove from the heat and cool completely.

Strain the simple syrup into a large bowl. Whisk in the mango puree and lime juice. Refrigerate the sorbet base for at least 4 hours; overnight is best.

Pour into an ice cream maker and churn according to the manufacturer's instructions. (If you don't have an ice cream maker, pour the mixture into a tall plastic container—a deli container works best—and freeze for 3 hours. Use an immersion blender to blend the mixture every 3 to 4 hours until set.) Freeze for 1 hour before serving.

# GRAPE CHAAT SORBET

This sorbet doesn't have a lot of added sugar since grapes are naturally so sweet! I like to serve this sorbet as a palate cleanser or as a treat after a chaat party! It's made with chaat masala, a mixture of spices like black salt, cumin, ginger, and more, which is spicy, sweet, and tart. Indians love their chattpata (mouthwatering) foods when sweet, spicy, salty, and tangy all are present!

MAKES 1 PINT (480 ML)

¼ cup (50 g) granulated sugar

⅓ cup (80 ml) water

4 cups (650 g) grapes (Cotton Candy, Muscat, and Concord varieties work best)

½ teaspoon chaat masala, plus more for sprinkling

¼ teaspoon kosher salt

Pinch of black salt (optional)

In a saucepan, bring the sugar and water to a boil and simmer until all the sugar has dissolved, about 2 minutes. Set the simple syrup aside to cool.

In a blender, combine the grapes, chaat masala, salt, and black salt (if using). Blend until smooth and strain into a bowl. Add the simple syrup and whisk until well combined. Refrigerate overnight.

Pour into an ice cream maker and churn according to the manufacturer's instructions. (If you don't have an ice cream maker, pour the mixture into a tall plastic container—a deli container works best—and freeze for 3 hours. Use an immersion blender to blend the mixture every 3 to 4 hours until set.)

Pour the sorbet into a container and freeze for at least 2 hours before serving.

Serve with a sprinkling of chaat masala.

# MANGO DOLLY SHORTCAKE BARS

My maternal grandmother had a love for ice cream that could rival my daughter Elara's. She'd often use me and my sister as an excuse to eat as many ice bars and ice pops as she could, and we loved her for it! When she lived with us, she'd pick me and my sister up from school and walk us home. In the summers she'd bring us popsicles or strawberry shortcake bars that we could enjoy on our way home. When she moved back to India, she'd sneak me and my sister money to go to the corner store and buy Chocobars and Mango Dollies. This is my little ode to her, taking my favorite part of an American strawberry shortcake bar, the crunch on the outside, and mashing it with creamy Mango Dolly (think orangesicles, but made with mango!).

This recipe is inspired by Serious Eats' Klondike bar recipe. I use aquafaba, the liquid from a can of chickpeas, to make it eggless. The ice cream is so light and fluffy! I also use Oreo Thins so that you don't have to worry about scraping the cream out of all those Oreos. In addition, you can find freeze-dried mangoes at Trader Joe's or online. For the white chocolate coating, use a good-quality chocolate like Lindt, Valrhona, or Ghirardelli; it really makes all the difference! I also used silicone molds for my bars, but you can make the ice cream, pour it into an 8-inch (20 cm) square pan, freeze it, cut it, and coat them in the chocolate and crunch.

MAKES 6 ICE CREAM BARS
(DEPENDING ON SIZE OF MOLD)

## MANGO CREAM ICE CREAM

⅓ cup (80 ml) concentrated aquafaba (page 15)

¼ teaspoon cream of tartar

¼ teaspoon kosher salt

7 tablespoons (88 g) granulated sugar

1 cup (240 ml) heavy cream

¼ teaspoon vanilla extract

½ cup (51 g) mango puree

## MANGO CRUNCH

1 cup (28 g) freeze-dried mango

10 Oreo Thins Golden sandwich cookies

Pinch of salt

2 tablespoons unsalted butter, melted

### FOR THE MANGO CREAM ICE CREAM

In a stand mixer fitted with the whisk, combine the aquafaba, cream of tartar, salt, and sugar and whisk on high until you have a stiff meringue, 10 to 15 minutes. Set aside.

In a separate bowl, whisk the heavy cream and vanilla until you reach stiff peaks, 4 to 5 minutes. Do not overmix this; otherwise, you will end up with butter!

Add the mango puree and one-third of the whipped cream to the aquafaba meringue and whisk until combined. Add the rest of the whipped cream and gently fold the mixture until well incorporated. You want to be extra gentle here so that you retain all that air that was whipped into the ice cream to make it fluffy.

Immediately spoon the mixture into ice pop molds and use a spatula or spoon to spread the mixture into an even layer. Freeze for at least 4 hours, but overnight is best.

### FOR THE MANGO CRUNCH

In a food processor, process the freeze-dried mango to fine crumbs. Add the Oreos and salt and process until you have small crumbs. Add the melted butter and mix until well combined. Pour into a small bowl and set aside. Line a sheet pan with foil and place in the freezer.

CONTINUED

## WHITE CHOCOLATE SHELL

7 ounces (200 g) good-quality white chocolate, chopped (1 cup)

½ cup (100 g) coconut oil

## FOR THE WHITE CHOCOLATE SHELL

In a microwave-safe bowl, combine the white chocolate and coconut oil and microwave in 15-second increments, mixing after each, until melted. Cool the mixture down until it is 80°F (27°C) or room temperature. Pour the chocolate into a tall glass that is wide enough for your ice cream bars.

Remove the ice cream bars from the molds; they are super delicate so be slow and gentle. Place the unmolded bars onto the prepared baking sheet in the freezer. Grabbing one ice cream bar at a time from the freezer, dip them into the chocolate until coated and then place into the bowl of mango crunch and use your hands to gently press the crunch mixture all over the bar. Work quickly as the chocolate sets fast. Return to the baking sheet and repeat until all the bars are coated. Freeze for 1 hour before enjoying.

# MASALA CHAI SEMIFREDDO

While recipe testing for this book, the amount of willpower I needed to not eat the whole pint of this in one sitting was immense! It's salty, sweet, creamy, and warm with spices—it's a star! Semifreddo is similar to ice cream, but it has a mousse-like, creamier texture since it's made with eggs. It doesn't need to be spun in an ice cream machine and instead sets into a soft, airy frozen dessert. For this recipe, don't use your fancy tea leaves; Lipton's black tea will work just fine.

Also, although semifreddo is not typically used for an affogato, I highly suggest pouring a shot of espresso or a little hot coffee on a scoop of this semifreddo for an extra special treat!

MAKES 1 PINT (480 ML)

¾ cup (180 ml) heavy cream

2 tablespoons CTC black tea leaves

½ teaspoon Chai Masala (page 24)

2 large eggs

6 tablespoons (75 g) granulated sugar

¼ teaspoon kosher salt

In a saucepan, combine the heavy cream, tea, and chai masala and bring to a boil. Remove from the heat, cover, and let the mixture cool completely.

Strain the cream into a bowl and whisk until you reach stiff peaks, 4 to 5 minutes. Do not overmix this; otherwise, you will end up with butter!

In a saucepan, combine the eggs, sugar, and salt and whisk over low heat until the mixture hits 165°F (74°C), 5 to 8 minutes. Remove from the heat and whisk until pale and fluffy.

Gently fold the whipped eggs and whipped cream into each other until well combined. Pour the mixture into five 4-ounce (115 ml) teacups, or a 1-pint (480 ml) container and freeze until set.

- - - - - - - - - - - - - - - - - - - - - - - - - - - - - - - - - - - - - - - - - - -

## MAKE IT EGGLESS

Increase the heavy cream to 1 cup (240 ml) and make the chai whipped cream as directed. Omit the eggs and sugar and whisk ⅓ cup (112 g) of sweetened condensed milk and the salt into the chai whipped cream until smooth and then freeze.

# Drinks

# HIBISCUS SHIKANJI

Shikanji is a cooling drink that's made with lemon or lime juice, cumin, and fennel. It has naturally cooling properties and helps balance your electrolytes after a hot day. For this recipe, I add hibiscus tea, which adds a tartness similar to limes! I love the deep red color of this drink! My hibiscus cooler can be made with hibiscus tea or fresh hibiscus buds. If you choose to add tequila to this cocktail, I recommend using 21 Seeds Hibiscus Grapefruit Tequila, but you can omit it entirely for a thirst-quenching nonalcoholic drink.

MAKES 4 TO 6 DRINKS

### SPICED SYRUP

1 cup (200 g) granulated sugar

1 cup (240 ml) water

4 star anise pods

½ teaspoon cumin seeds, coarsely crushed

½ teaspoon fennel seeds, coarsely crushed

### HIBISCUS TEA

2 cups (480 ml) water

2 tablespoons hibiscus tea or 6 fresh hibiscus buds

### DRINK

¼ cup (60 ml) fresh lemon juice

¾ cup (180 ml) tequila (optional)

Lemon wedges and coarse salt, for rimming the glasses

Ice

### FOR THE SPICED SYRUP

In a saucepan, combine the sugar, water, star anise, cumin seeds, and fennel seeds and bring to a boil over medium-high heat. Reduce to a simmer and cook until all the sugar has dissolved, about 2 minutes. Remove from the heat, cover, and steep the syrup for 10 minutes. Strain and set aside.

### FOR THE HIBISCUS TEA

In a saucepan, boil the water. Add the hibiscus tea and steep for 6 to 7 minutes. Strain into a large pitcher.

### FOR THE DRINK

Add the lemon juice, tequila (if using), and spiced syrup to taste to the hibiscus tea. Stir well.

To serve, rub a lemon onto the rims of your cups and dip the rims in coarse salt. Fill the cups with ice and then pour in the shikanji and serve.

# COLD COCO

Until I went to Surat to do research for this book, I had never heard of cold coco. I saw stalls selling cold coco everywhere in Surat, advertising how their coco is the creamiest, richest, and coldest! Cold coco is a thick and creamy cocoa that is served ice cold. It has the consistency of a melted milkshake and tastes like Hershey's chocolate syrup (which is what I'm pretty sure they use). Here is my upgraded version that's not too sweet and hits all the rich chocolaty notes! I wanted the drink to be rich but not feel too slick in your mouth, so I used more milk than cream and added a dollop of whipped cream to make it a bit more lush!

MAKES 6 SERVINGS

## COLD COCO

¼ cup (21 g) unsweetened cocoa powder

⅔ cup (74 g) powdered sugar

½ teaspoon vanilla extract

½ teaspoon kosher salt

½ cup (120 ml) heavy cream

2¾ cups (671 g) whole milk

½ cup (80 g) chopped dark chocolate

## CHOCOLATE WHIPPED CREAM

½ cup (120 ml) heavy cream

½ cup (60 g) powdered sugar

2 teaspoons unsweetened cocoa powder

Grated chocolate, for garnish (optional)

## COLD COCO

In a saucepan, combine the cocoa powder, powdered sugar, vanilla, salt, and heavy cream and stir with a whisk until you have a smooth mixture. Add half the milk and bring to a boil over medium-high heat. Once it boils, remove the saucepan from the heat and stir in the chopped chocolate and stir until all the chocolate has melted and you have a smooth mixture. Whisk in the rest of the milk and chill in the refrigerator.

## FOR THE CHOCOLATE WHIPPED CREAM

In a stand mixer fitted with the whisk, beat the heavy cream, powdered sugar, and cocoa powder on high speed until stiff peaks form, 5 to 6 minutes. Do not overmix this; otherwise, you will end up with butter!

Pour the chilled coco into glasses and dollop with chocolate whipped cream and a little grated chocolate, if you're feeling fancy, and serve!

# PASSION FRUIT JAL JEERA

Here's a tropical take on jal jeera! Jal jeera is a savory, sweet drink made with lime juice, cumin, black salt, and a touch of sugar. It's tart, salty, sweet, and one of my favorite drinks! For the passion fruit juice, I used fresh passion fruit pulp, but you can use passion fruit juice as well! The recipe for the jal jeera masala will make more than you need, so save it to make more drinks! I like to add it to lemon-lime sodas, cut up fruit, or cucumbers!

**MAKES 6 SERVINGS**

12 to 15 fresh mint leaves

1 tablespoon sugar

4½ teaspoons Jal Jeera Masala (recipe follows), plus more for sprinkling

1½ cups (360 ml) water

6 tablespoons (90 ml) fresh lime juice

Lime wedges and coarse salt, for rimming the glasses

6 tablespoons (90 ml) passion fruit pulp or juice

Ice

Mint sprigs, for garnish

In a large pitcher or bowl, combine the mint leaves, sugar, and 4 teaspoons of the jal jeera masala. Use the bottom of a spatula or a muddler to muddle the mint leaves into the sugar and spices. Add the water and lime juice and mix well.

On a small plate, mix together 1 tablespoon kosher or coarse salt and the remaining ½ teaspoon jal jeera masala. Rub a lime wedge onto the rims of six cups and coat the rims in the jal jeera salt. Add 1 tablespoon of passion fruit pulp or juice to the bottom of each cup and fill with ice.

Strain the lime jal jeera mixture into each cup until filled. Sprinkle a little extra jal jeera masala on top of each drink, garnish with mint, and enjoy!

- - - - - - - - - - - - - - - - - - - - - - - - - - - - - - - - - - -

**NOTE**

- If you want to make a big pitcher instead, add the passion fruit juice along with the lime juice and stir well!

**JAL JEERA MASALA**

In a small bowl, combine 1½ tablespoons of dark brown sugar, 1 tablespoon of amchur (green mango powder), 1 tablespoon of ground cumin, 2 teaspoons of dried mint, 1½ teaspoons of red chile powder (optional), 1 teaspoon of ground ginger, ¾ teaspoon of black salt (kala namak) or chaat masala, ½ teaspoon freshly of ground black pepper, and 1½ teaspoons of kosher salt and whisk to combine. This makes about ¼ cup (40 g) of jal jeera masala. Sprinkle in your lemonade/limeade or lime soda!

# STRAWBERRY ROSE FALOODA

Falooda is the queen of all fancy dessert drinks. It's normally made with rose syrup, milk, vermicelli noodles, basil seeds, and sometimes ice cream! It's a beautiful drink with various shades of pinks and reds! For my version, I make a strawberry jelly and add that to the bottom to mimic grass jelly drinks that I get from my local boba shops! Also, if you don't have rose syrup, you can also use Rooh Afza, a brand of rose-based syrup you can find at your local Indian store. This dessert is a party of textures, and it has a lovely light floral and fruity flavor.

MAKES 4 SERVINGS

### STRAWBERRY JELLY

1 cup (240 ml) strawberry juice

2 tablespoons granulated sugar

¾ teaspoon agar-agar

### FALOODA

1 tablespoon basil seeds (tukmaria), plus more for garnish

½ cup (120 ml) water

½ cup (22 g) vermicelli noodles (falooda sev), wheat or cornstarch

2 cups (480 ml) whole milk

4 to 6 tablespoons (60 to 90 ml) Rose Syrup (page 24)

1 cup (214 g) vanilla ice cream

### FOR THE STRAWBERRY JELLY

In a saucepan, combine the strawberry juice, sugar, and agar-agar and bring to a boil. Boil for 3 minutes, then pour the liquid into a shallow container that is at least 1 inch (2.5 cm) deep. Place in the fridge to set.

### FOR THE FALOODA

In a small bowl, stir together the basil seeds and water and set aside for 20 minutes.

Cook the vermicelli noodles according to the package directions. Drain well and set aside.

In a large, spouted measuring cup, combine the milk and rose syrup (add more or less to your taste) and mix well.

Cut the set strawberry jelly into ¼-inch (6 mm) cubes and spoon them into the bottom of four tall glasses. Top with the cooked vermicelli noodles. Divide the rose milk evenly among the four glasses and top with the ice cream and 1 to 2 teaspoons of basil seeds and additional strawberry jelly.

# PINEAPPLE AAM PANNA

Aam panna is a drink made from boiled raw or green mango and a few spices. It's normally made in the summers as a cooling refresher. This is another salty-sweet drink that really just quenches your thirst and hits the spot on a hot day. This recipe makes an aam panna concentrate, which you dilute with cold water. I like to make a batch of this and keep it in the fridge for up to a week. You want to use hard, unripe green mangoes for this recipe as you want the tartness that they bring for the drink!

MAKES 4 TO 5 DRINKS

1 green mango

1½ cups (240 g) chopped fresh pineapple

5 to 6 fresh mint leaves

2⅓ cups (455 g) granulated sugar

¾ teaspoon black salt (kala namak) or chaat masala

¼ teaspoon kosher salt

¼ teaspoon freshly ground black pepper

½ teaspoon ground cumin

Mint sprigs and pineapple wedges (optional), for garnish

In a saucepan, combine the mango (unpeeled) with water to cover. Bring to a boil over medium-high heat and cook until the mango is soft and tender, about 1 hour, topping with hot water when needed.

Drain the mango and let cool. Peel and spoon the pulp from the cooked mango into a blender. Add the pineapple, mint leaves, sugar, black salt, salt, black pepper, and cumin and blend until smooth.

To make a drink, stir 3 to 4 tablespoons (45 to 60 ml) of the pineapple aam panna concentrate into 1 cup (240 ml) of ice-cold water and mix well before serving. Garnish with a mint sprig and pineapple wedge, if desired.

# GRAPEFRUIT & FENNEL SHARBAT

Sharbat is a cold drink made with a mix of fruit juices and sometimes spices. Think of it as an Indian punch! My family would make sharbat during special occasions or parties since it's super easy to throw together!

I know many of my drink recipes include fennel; this is because it has natural cooling properties and adds a natural sweetness to drinks. Try it out: Chew a few fennel seeds and drink some plain water. You'll see that the water tastes a little sweet!

MAKES 6 DRINKS

## FENNEL SIMPLE SYRUP

½ cup (100 g) granulated sugar

½ cup (120 ml) water

2 teaspoons fennel seeds, coarsely crushed

## SHARBAT (PER DRINK)

1½ ounces (45 ml) grapefruit juice

1 ounce (30 ml) fresh lime juice

1 ounce (30 ml) simple syrup

Ice

Sparkling water, for topping up

Fennel fronds and a ruby grapefruit wedge, for garnish

### FOR THE FENNEL SIMPLE SYRUP

In a saucepan, combine the sugar, water, and fennel seeds and bring to a boil. Simmer for 1 minute and strain. Cool completely.

### FOR ONE DRINK

Add the grapefruit juice, lime juice, and simple syrup to a cup and mix well. Add ice and top up with sparkling water. Garnish with fennel fronds and a grapefruit wedge.

## NOTE

• Add 1 ounce (30 ml) of tequila to make a delicious paloma!

# ROSE COLD BREW

I'm not a coffee drinker, but I do love a good cold brew with lots of milk! This rose cold brew is topped with rose sweet cream that just melts into your cold brew, sweetening it and adding a lovely floral aroma and flavor!

MAKES 7 SERVINGS

## CONCENTRATE

¾ cup (88 g) coffee beans

3½ cups (840 ml) cold water

¼ cup (4 g) dried rose petals

## ROSE SWEET CREAM

2 cups (480 ml) half-and-half

7 tablespoons (137 g) sweetened condensed milk

¾ teaspoon rose water, store-bought or homemade (page 23)

¾ teaspoon vanilla extract

### FOR THE CONCENTRATE

Grind the coffee beans and add the ground coffee beans to a jar with the water and dried rose petals. Refrigerate overnight. Strain the mixture and pour it into a clean jar. This cold-brew concentrate can be refrigerated for 1 week.

### FOR THE ROSE SWEET CREAM

In a container, stir together the half-and-half, condensed milk, rose water, and vanilla. This sweet cream can be refrigerated for 1 week.

To make your coffee, fill a cup with ice and add one part cold brew concentrate and one part water. Mix well and add rose sweet cream to your taste.

# MANGO-APRICOT JUICE

This drink can be made to mimic Maaza or Frooti! Maaza is a brand of thick mango juice, which was always a treat whenever I'd go to Patel Brothers, an Indian grocery store chain in the United States, with my family as a kid. Frooti is a brand of mango juice that is thinner and comes in juice boxes and often made an appearance in my lunch boxes growing up. For this juice, I use ripe apricots and mango, but if you want to keep it classic, you can just use more mangoes instead. I highly recommend using Honey or Ataulfo mangoes for this recipe as they have little fiber and are super sweet!

MAKES 4 TO 6 SERVINGS

2 mangoes, cubed

4 fresh apricots, pitted and cut into large pieces

¼ cup (50 g) granulated sugar

1 cup (240 ml) water

2 tablespoons fresh lemon juice

Pinch of salt

In a saucepan, combine the mangoes, apricots, sugar, and water and bring to a boil. Simmer for 15 minutes.

Transfer the mixture to a blender and blend until smooth. Add the lemon juice and salt and blend until smooth. Strain the mixture into a pitcher and add enough chilled water until it reaches a consistency you like. About ¾ cup (180 ml) chilled water will create a nice thick Maaza-like consistency; add more for a thinner juice like Frooti!

# MANGO JAM LIMONCELLO SPRITZER

Jam spritzers are my favorite lazy girl drinks. Just add jam and sparkling water to a cup and mix, and you have an easy drink! For this, I use homemade mango jam and add a little limoncello to it to make it a bit more interesting. If you're not feeling the alcohol, you can use lemon juice instead; just add an additional tablespoon of murabba to help sweeten it a bit.

**MAKES 2 DRINKS**

5 to 6 fresh mint leaves

1 teaspoon sugar

¼ cup (60 ml) limoncello

2 tablespoons Mango Murabba (page 27)

Edible glitter (optional)

Ice

Sparkling water, for topping up

Mint sprigs, for garnish

In a cocktail shaker, combine the mint leaves and sugar and muddle. Add the limoncello, mango jam, and edible glitter (if using) and shake well. Strain and pour the mixture even into two ice-filled glasses. Top up with sparkling water and garnish with a mint sprig.

# ACKNOWLEDGMENTS

This book has been a labor of love, and it would not have been possible without the help of so many people! Thank you to my parents who shared their love of food and art with me. They showed me the importance of making things with your hands and putting yourself into your work, whether it be a cake or a piece of jewelry. To my sister, my permanent sous-chef for life, thanks for joining me on this journey and letting me boss you around India and listening to all my ideas and vetoing them as needed. I truly don't think I would have survived India, or life, without you. To my husband, Rhut, thanks for letting me shove tons of food into your mouth and giving me your honest opinions. You make me a better baker and cook. Also thank you for taking Elara on a whole summer adventure so that I could hyperfixate on this book! I'm grateful to my in-laws Tarak and Dipti, for supporting me and always being my biggest cheerleaders and also letting Rhut and Elara spend their summer with them while I worked away at home. Elara, your excitement for licking smashulas and helping me bake brings me so much joy! I can't wait to see all the art and food you create as you get older!

Also big thanks to Manasvi and Gaurav and their massive textile collection. Thank you for letting me borrow all your gorgeous fabrics! To Pehramni, for showing me all your beautiful Kutchi handicrafts and keeping the art going and providing me with so much inspiration. Thanks to Ananya and Shruti for helping me recipe test all the recipes and spending your summer baking in my kitchen with me! And to my friends who served as enthusiastic taste testers throughout the journey.

To Amy, thank you so much for rooting for this book! Your confidence in me and my vision has been beyond amazing, and I appreciate it so much!

Thank you, Jenny Wapner and the team at Hardie Grant for taking a chance on my cookbook! To the copyeditors, thank you for dealing with my typos and bouts of my keyboard dyslexia.

Last but not least, to all my followers and supporters, a second book would not have been in the works if it weren't for you guys! Thank you so much for baking my recipes, sharing them with your friends and families, and supporting me in all my endeavors. I am forever grateful and lucky to be able to do what I do because of you.

# INDEX

**Hardie Grant**

P U B L I S H I N G

Hardie Grant North America

2912 Telegraph Ave

Berkeley, CA 94705

hardiegrantusa.com

Published in the United States by Hardie Grant
North America, an imprint of Hardie Grant
Publishing Pty Ltd.

Library of Congress Cataloging-in-Publication
Data is available upon request.

ISBN: 9781958417317

ISBN: 9781958417324 (eBook)

Printed in China

Design by Swasti Mittal

First Edition

MIX
Paper | Supporting
responsible forestry
FSC® C020056
FSC
www.fsc.org

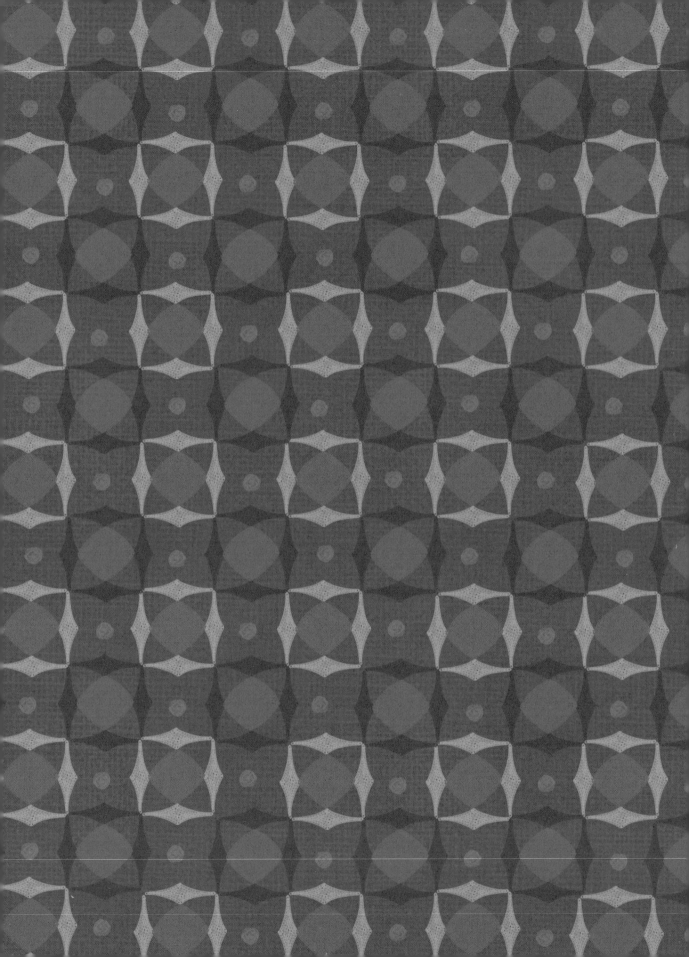